NORTH CAROLINA
IN THE
CIVIL WAR

NORTH CAROLINA
IN THE
CIVIL WAR

MICHAEL C. HARDY

Charleston · London

THE
History
PRESS

Published by The History Press
Charleston, SC 29403
www.historypress.net

Front Cover, top: Recently freed slaves entering New Bern, *Harpers Weekly*; *bottom*: Capture of
Fort Fisher, *Library of Congress*
Back Cover, top: The Lawrence O'Bryan Branch Drum and Fife Corps, *North Carolina Museum
of History*; *bottom*: Salisbury Prison, *North Carolina Museum of History*.
First published 2011

Manufactured in the United States

ISBN 978.1.60949.106.2

Library of Congress Cataloging-in-Publication Data

Hardy, Michael C.
North Carolina in the Civil War / Michael C. Hardy.
p. cm.
Includes bibliographical references.
ISBN 978-1-60949-106-2
1. North Carolina--History--Civil War, 1861-1865. I. Title.
E524.H37 2011
975.6'03--dc23
2011021183

Contents

Preface

S ince World War II, there has been an explosion in the number of books, articles and dissertations on North Carolina's role in our great national calamity, the American Civil War. Much of this research has greatly deepened our understanding of what took place in the 1860s. Surprisingly, only once has a concise history been undertaken. In 1987, the North Carolina Department of Archives and History published Dr. John G. Barrett's *North Carolina as a Civil War Battleground.* This new book fills the void that has been left: it provides a condensed history of the role of North Carolina and the Civil War. On the other hand, this volume goes beyond the war, providing a broader examination than that of Barrett's 1987 work. There is a chapter on the soldiers who marched away and fought on distant fields of battles; one that examines both presidential and congressional reconstruction in North Carolina; and a chapter on the memorial practices that took place in North Carolina in the decades following the war. No other one text tackles all these goals.

A full examination of the scholarship dealing with North Carolina and the war would take a volume this size. It is sufficient to say that consulting the bibliography in this book would be a great start on matters concerning the war as a whole, the war in different sections of the state, regimental histories and time-period-specific histories, like Reconstruction.

There is more to understanding the war than simply reading words on a printed page. By visiting museums and historic sites, you can see and come in contact with visible pieces of our past: instruments of war like rifles and cannon, tattered uniforms and blood-soaked flags. Visiting places like the Vance Birthplace just north of Asheville, the Museum of History in Raleigh or Fort Macon along the coast can add greatly to our understanding of the time period.

There are many people whom the author wishes to thank. First and foremost would be all of those other historians, like Barrett, Trotter, Inscoe, McKinney, Bradley, Zuber…this list could go on and on. These oft-read historians make compiling a history such as this a much simpler task. The hard part has been condensing the information. The author would also like to thank Jessica Berzon at The History Press for all of her help and, most importantly, Elizabeth, Nathaniel and Isabella for all the time they spent traveling from one end of the state to the other, tramping battlefields and checking out museums. Our lives are, I believe, richer for the experience.

Chapter 1

On the Homefront
1861

C urious spectators watched the trail of the burning fuse as it arced across the sky toward Fort Sumter. Numerous North Carolinians had joined their neighbors in Charleston, South Carolina, to watch the opening salvos of what would prove a costly war. One North Carolinian, who had ventured from Wilmington just to watch the bombardment, wrote, "But see! from a point on the right a white puff of smoke is sent, and, ere the report reaches us, a red flame bursts over the flag staff of Fort Sumter and the dreadful bomb scatters its fragments over the doomed fort...The result of the conflict strengthens and confirms our faith in the justness of the course." A few days later, the editor of the *Fayetteville Observer* wrote: "This is dreadful news. War is a terrible evil. Civil war the worst of all earthly evils. Nothing but dire necessity can justify it...The stake is too great to rush into disunion and civil war upon the strength of telegraphic dispatches. In the mean time it will do no harm to be cool, calmly looking the great crisis in the face." It was an opinion shared by many in North Carolina for months prior to April 12, 1861. Now, the *Fayetteville Observer* was in the minority.

Debate about secession had festered for decades. The New England states threatened secession over the election of Thomas Jefferson in 1800 and again in 1814–15, in what became known as the Hartford Convention, over the War of 1812. South Carolina, in 1832, declared that the Federal Tariffs of 1828 and 1832 were unconstitutional and null and void within the state, a process that could easily have led to secession. Once again, New England threatened secession during the War with Mexico in the 1840s, and in the 1850s, many in the South raised the call to withdraw from the Union. All of these movements have one central element in common: the perceived power of the Federal government. It was that same dispute that led South Carolina to leave the Union and to fire on Fort Sumter.

On center stage was the question of how far the Federal government should intervene in the role of state governments and individual citizens. Many in the South, and a few in the North, believed that the role of the government should be limited. It was a debate that raged throughout the 1850s, and many believed that the Union could be torn asunder at any time. Much of the debate in the 1850s centered on the ownership of slaves. Slave ownership was legal in the colonies for one hundred years prior to the creation of the United States, and all of the original colonies had allowed the system. Gradually, the Northern states had realized that the institution was not profitable, and Northern slave owners had sold or emancipated their chattel. By 1860, the slave population had grown to four million, mostly located in the South. However, slavery was a national system. The textile mills in the North, fueling the Industrial Revolution in the United States, depended on slave labor in the South to provide raw materials.

North Carolina had a population in 1860 of 992,622 people, of which 331,059 were enslaved. A little over 27 percent of the population owned slaves, including 8 free persons of color who owned 25 men and women. Geographically, North Carolina was divided into three regions. The eastern portion of the state, along the coast, was the wealthiest, containing large plantations that grew primarily rice, tobacco and cotton. Eastern North Carolina contained twenty of the thirty-six banks in the state, nine cotton mills (with seven alone in Cumberland County) and the only deepwater port: Wilmington. With a population of 9,552, Wilmington was the largest city in the state, followed by New Bern, Fayetteville and Raleigh, all located in the east. The Piedmont section of North Carolina was home to a combination of eastern planters, especially in counties that bordered Virginia and South Carolina, and yeoman farmers, frequently found farther west. For the latter, principal crops included grains and livestock. There were 1,206 manufacturing establishments in Piedmont North Carolina, including thirty textile mills and thirteen banks. Charlotte was the largest city in this section of the state. Only 8 percent of the population could qualify as members of the planter class, owning 20 or more slaves. Thomasville, in Davidson County, was one of the up-and-coming leaders of the central portion of North Carolina, boasting not only a coach maker, wagon maker and brickyard but also the C.M. & George Lines Shoe

On the Homefront: 1861

William W. Avery, from Burke County, introduced the resolution that split the Democratic convention in 1860. *North Carolina Museum of History*.

Factory, thought to be the largest shoe manufacturer in the South. In the eastern and central portions of the North Carolina, there were almost nine hundred miles of railroad. Western North Carolina, with its foothills and mountains, comprised the third section. Writing just one year after the war, Randolph Shotwell believed that "probably no section of the state contains a population so widely diversified in politics, wealth, morals, and general intelligence." There were only 192 manufacturing establishments in western North Carolina, but the area had produced one of the first gold rushes in the nation. Enslaved people made up just 10 percent of the population, with slave owners also numbering just 10 percent. Instead of planters being the largest slave owners, in western North Carolina they were merchants, doctors and lawyers. Tourism was already a flourishing trade, with Flat Rock and Hendersonville drawing visitors from places as far away as Charleston. Livestock, namely cattle, sheep and hogs, was the principal crop. Asheville, Rutherfordton and Morganton were the principal towns.

Across the state, as well as across the nation, no other event in the history of the United States proved as divisive as the 1860 presidential election. At the convention in Charleston, South Carolina, in April 1860, the Democratic (Conservative) Party split over the party's platform. The platform chair was Burke County native William W. Avery, who believed that a Federal slave code was mandatory. Many Northern members of the party would not agree, and the delegates from the lower states walked out of the convention. A second convention met in Baltimore in June, but that convention also met opposition. In the end, those left at the Baltimore convention nominated Vice President John C. Breckinridge for president. The Northern branch of the Democratic Party nominated Stephen Douglas for president. A third group, the Constitutional Union Party, whose platform was simply to support the Constitution and the Union, nominated John Bell for president. Lastly, the new Republican Party (liberal), with a platform that "all men were created equal" and that "freedom was the natural state of any territory," nominated Abraham Lincoln for president. When the votes from the election, held in November 1860, were tallied, Breckinridge won the state, with 48,538 votes, and Bell came in second with 44,990 votes. Only 2,701 men cast a vote for Douglas. The Republican Party had so few supporters in North Carolina that Lincoln was not even able to get on the ballot. However, while only gaining 40 percent of the overall national vote, Lincoln gained a majority of the Electoral College, and the Illinois lawyer became the sixteenth president. Many in North Carolina advocated a "watch and wait" policy, believing that the election of a Republican was not sufficient cause for secession.

South Carolinians wasted little time. Meeting on December 20, delegates unanimously voted to secede. When news of secession reached Wilmington, a local militia company fired a 101-gun salute, which was echoed by the schooner *Marina*, at anchor in the Cape Fear River. South Carolina was followed by Mississippi, Florida, Alabama, Georgia, Louisiana and Texas, all seceding from the Union. On February 4, delegates from these states met in Montgomery, Alabama, forming a provisional Confederate government and electing Mississippian Jefferson Davis, a former secretary of war and United States senator, as provisional president. On February 8, they adopted a provisional constitution.

North Carolina was literally torn asunder. The first meeting advocating secession was held in Cleveland County on November 12, 1860. Union meetings soon followed. Many counties, cities and towns had both. Wilmington citizens originally had the meetings scheduled for the same day, but since most citizens wanted to attend both, they were rescheduled, with the union meeting on December 11 and the secession meeting on December 12.

Three different factions developed in North Carolina. The Unionists were unequivocally opposed to secession. Conditional Unionists were against secession if the rights of the South were guaranteed. And lastly, Secessionists were for the immediate withdrawal from the Union. Many politicians

John W. Ellis served as governor of North Carolina until his death in 1861. He was replaced by Henry T. Clark. *North Carolina Museum of History*.

canvassed their districts campaigning for one of the positions. Two North Carolina congressmen, Thomas Ruffin from Rockingham County and Burton Craige from Rowan County, believed that "all hope of relief in the Union…is extinguished." Some, like Congressman Zebulon Vance from Buncombe County, were opposed to disunion while at the same time, in private correspondence, advocating splitting the United States up into several different countries. One politician remembered that Vance "engaged in a kind of campaign resembling a religious revival…He appeared in churches, even at street corners, shouting always: 'Keep North Carolina in the Union! Let it not follow the example of other Southern States!'" Vance's Unionism was so pronounced that Secessionists in Yancey County hanged him in effigy in January 1861.

The governor of North Carolina in 1860–61 was forty-year-old John W. Ellis, a Secessionist leader from Rowan County. In his message to the legislation in December 1860, Ellis believed that Lincoln's election endangered the rights of Southerners and that a convention of North Carolinians should be called to consider the question of secession and that the state must start preparing the military. The General Assembly agreed and, on January 24, 1861, passed a bill calling for a vote on whether to call a convention and to elect delegates based on their representation in the House of Commons. Active campaigning by Secessionists and Unionists was fierce. Three of the leading newspapers in the state, the Raleigh-based *North Carolina Standard*, the *Raleigh Register* and the *Fayetteville Observer*, were all opposed to secession. Union and secession meetings continued across the state. On February 1, in Ansonville, locals raised a Secessionist flag. Such flag-raisings occurred in other communities across the state as well.

Men gathered at the polls on February 28 and cast 47,322 votes against calling the convention, and with 46,672 for the convention, a margin of 650 votes kept North Carolina in the Union. While the majority against calling a convention was slim, Unionists did not have much cause to rejoice. News filtered into the Tar Heel State that on February 27, the Peace Commission in Washington, D.C., to which North Carolina had sent delegates, had failed. Lincoln's inaugural address on March 4 did little to alleviate concerns in the state and might have even driven some from the Union and into the Secessionists' ranks. In late March, the Southern Rights, or State Rights, Party was formed in Goldsboro, and meetings quickly took shape elsewhere. Original Secessionists like Thomas L. Clingman backed the movement, and soon others, like Congressman Lawrence Branch, joined. In the United States Senate, Thomas Bragg withdrew his seat on March 6, followed by Clingman on March 28. Both were later expelled from the Senate in July 1861.

April 1861 was a pivotal month. On the twelfth, Confederate forces in Charleston opened fire on Fort Sumter, which capitulated on April 13. Lincoln issued a proclamation on April 15 declaring that an insurrection existed and requested that the states call up 75,000 militia. North Carolina's quota was 1,500. "Your dispatch is received," Governor Ellis telegraphed back, "and if genuine, which its extraordinary character leads me to doubt, I have to say in reply, that I regard the levy of troops made by the administration for the purpose of subjugating the state of the South, as in violation of the Constitution, and as a gross usurpation of power. I can be no party to this violation of the laws of the country and to this war upon liberties of a free people. You can get no troops from North Carolina."

Ellis moved quickly. He ordered the forts along the coast seized. Forts Caswell and Johnston, near Wilmington, had been seized early in January 1861, but Ellis had ordered the overzealous militiamen to return the property to the caretakers. These forts, along with Fort Macon near Morehead City, were not even garrisoned by troops. Fort Macon was captured on April 14 by the Beaufort Harbor Guards. Two days later, the militia captured both Fort

Caswell on Oak Island and Fort Johnston near Southport. Fort Johnston was an earthen fort that had its beginnings during the mid-1700s. Forts Macon and Caswell were both masonry fortifications completed in 1836. The militia companies that captured the forts found all of them in a sad state of disrepair. Local militiamen also captured the Federal arsenal in Fayetteville on April 17, along with thirty-seven thousand muskets, and the Charlotte Greys captured the United States Mint in Charlotte on April 20. On the day the arsenal fell, Ellis ordered the state legislation into special session.

The capture of Fort Sumter, followed by Lincoln's proclamation and subsequent call for troops, electrified North Carolina. Zebulon Vance was in the midst of "canvassing for the Union...addressing a large and excited crowd...and literally had my hand extended upward in pleading for peace and the Union...when the telegraphic news was announced of the firing on Sumter and the president's call...When my hand came down from that impassioned gesticulation, it slowly and sadly fell by the side of a Secessionist." The Greensboro *Patriot* reported that on April 23, the "streets were filled with an excited crowd. They were addressed by Mr. J.W. Thomas of Davidson, Governor Morehead, Hon. R.C. Puryear, Hon. J.A. Gilmer, Ralph Gorrell, Esq., Samuel P. Hill, J.R. McLean, R.P. Dick, Thomas Settle and perhaps others. The speeches of these gentlemen all breathed the true spirit of resistance to tyrants, and that the time had come for North Carolina

Delegates met in the state capitol in Raleigh in May 1861 and voted to remove North Carolina from the Union. *North Carolina State Archives.*

to make a common cause with the brethren of the South." A few still held to their Unionist views. Bartholomew Moore of Raleigh wrote that "Civil. War can be glorious to none but demons or thoughtless fools, or maddened men."

On May 1, the General Assembly met, with the house unanimously passing a bill calling for an election of 120 delegates on May 13 and then a convention to meet in Raleigh on May 20. The Senate then passed the same bill, with three dissenting votes. In most counties in North Carolina, there were no clearly defined parties, with many of the Secessionist candidates running unopposed. The group that met on May 20 has been considered "one of the ablest political bodies ever assembled in North Carolina." Chairman of the convention was Weldon Edwards of Warrenton. Burton Craige of Rowan County introduced the ordinance of secession, which was unanimously adopted. A little after 5:30 p.m., a man stepped out onto the west balcony of the state capitol and dropped a white handkerchief: North Carolina had withdrawn from the Union. The crowd shouted, bells began to peal and Captain Stephen D. Ramseur ordered the Ellis Light Artillery to fire a salute. According to one postwar account, the concussion of the artillery shattered the glass windows along Fayetteville Street.

After passing the ordinance of secession, the delegates then ratified the provisional constitution of the Confederate States of America, at the same time defeating a motion that ratification of the document be placed before the people. On May 21, all 120 delegates signed the secession ordinance. The General Assembly authorized Ellis to spend $5 million on war materials, which Ellis quickly did, and then returned to ask for an additional $6.5 million. Various positions were created, like surgeon general, filled by Raleigh physician Charles Johnson, and quartermaster general, filled by former Congressman Lawrence Branch. Work, begun a month earlier, continued on coastal fortifications at Wilmington and along the Outer Banks.

Thousands of men rallied around the colors. Some were already in local, social companies, like the Ellis Light Artillery from Raleigh or the German Volunteers from Wilmington. Some of these companies had been in existence for a long time, while others had been formed after John Brown's raid on Harpers Ferry, Virginia. Others were part of local militia companies. According to the law, each county in the state had a militia regiment, with the county divided up into militia districts, each composing a company. Each regiment was scheduled to meet once a year for drill, although these drills often turned into social events with grand dinners and, at times, drunken brawls. However inadequate, these militias served as the backbone of the

The Confederate Grays, from Duplin County, were just one of many militia companies to offer their services to the state in May and June 1861. *North Carolina State Archives.*

new companies being formed. Most in these companies that were created in April and May 1861 were young men, ages eighteen to twenty-nine, literate and unmarried. They often enlisted out of a sense of adventure, believing that the war would end in three months with one grand battle. In many instances, these companies adopted grandiose names, like the Black River Tigers, the Bladen Stars, Brunswick Double Quicks, Cabarrus Hornets, Dixie Invincibles, General Bragg Guards, Haw River Boys, Mecklenburg Wide Awakes, Pee Dee Wide Wild Cats, Sandy Run Yellow Jackets, Sons of Mars and the Stanly Yankee Hunters.

In the early days of the war, experiences were typically the same. If one lived in a large town, a newspaper or a poster might announce the formation of a new company. In someplace rural, the announcement was often word of mouth. Harvey Davis, from Watauga County, enlisted on May 11, 1861, nine days before the state left the Union. Davis wrote in his diary about enlistment day. A local lawyer, and former congressman, George N. Folk, made a "some-what fiery speech" on the streets of Boone, dwelling on the attempts of the "North to dominate the South and abrogate her rights under the Constitution." At the end of the speech, Folk called for volunteers. This group chose to call themselves the Watauga Rangers, and Folk became captain. The new company was drilled for four weeks in Watauga County. All the while, the men "were invited and partook of several public banquets, set by the hospitable citizens of the county...we passed our time very enjoyable with the local citizens." Before long, Davis and the others found themselves in Asheville, and the Watauga Rangers were soon mustered in as Company D, 1st North Carolina Cavalry. Many of these companies were presented with flags on their departure. The Forsyth Rifles, destined to become Company D, 21st North Carolina State Troops, were presented a Confederate First National flag made by local ladies. Many of these flags were made from silk clothing, often donated by wives and daughters of company commanders. In Rutherford County, citizens gathered in front of a local hotel, and the Burnt Chimney Volunteers, which became Company D, 16th North Carolina State Troops, were presented a banner constructed

Many companies received handmade flags from the ladies before leaving for the war. This Confederate First National variant was presented to the Gaston Blues. *Author's collection.*

by the ladies of Rutherfordton. The banner was inscribed in gilt letters with "In God We Trust" on one side and "Victory or Death" on the other. After taking possession of the flag, the soldiers gave three cheers for the ladies.

Often, the soldiers were given bounties to help entice them into service. Transylvania County, one of the three new counties in North Carolina created in 1861, at the meeting of the first county court in May, voted to give each new soldier a bounty of fifteen dollars. Onslow County commissioners voted to give each volunteer a five-dollar bounty when he marched away.

North Carolina's Confederate soldiers were not all Anglo nor even all Southern. Men from just about every continent on the earth served in Tar Heel regiments. Company A of the 18th North Carolina Troops might have been the most cosmopolitan company from the state, with fifty-six men from Germany, Prussia or Bavaria and a smattering of men from France, England, Luxembourg and Denmark. Company D of the 7th North Carolina State Troops contained men from five countries, chiefly Ireland, and seven states besides North Carolina, including New York and Pennsylvania. There were some free persons of color who volunteered for Confederate service, including brothers William Henry and Franklin Cousins, who served in Company B, 37th North Carolina Troops. Franklin was killed in action on August 27, 1862. Then there was a legion recruited by William H. Thomas in 1862 containing hundreds of Cherokee Indians from Jackson, Cherokee and Haywood Counties

These new-made soldiers all needed someplace to go. The state fairgrounds in Raleigh was converted into a military camp, known as Camp Ellis, and placed under the command of Colonel Daniel H. Hill, superintendent of the North Carolina Military Institute in Charlotte. Soon, the cadets from the institute were on hand to serve as drillmasters for the new recruits. Two additional camps were created to handle the influx of men: Camp Mangum was four miles from Raleigh, near the railroad, and Camp Crabtree was several miles north of the city. The soldiers had to adapt to a routine schedule. One soldier recorded life at Camp Magnum: "Reveille at Daybreak, Breakfast call at 6½ a.m. Sick call at 7 a.m. Guard Mounting at 730 a.m. Squad Drill from 8 to 9 a.m. Company Drill from 10 to 12 m. Orderly Call 12 m Dinner call at 12½ p.m. Battalion Drill from 3 to 430 p.m. Dress Parade at 530 p.m. Tattoo at 8 p.m. [and] Taps at 830 p.m." Other camps sprang up across the state, like Camp Patton in Asheville and Camp Fisher in High Point. Many of the soldiers were issued the old muskets that had been captured in the arsenal in Fayetteville. To a large extent, these weapons were flintlocks that needed to be converted to the percussion system. When the 37th North Carolina Troops was issued flintlocks, the regimental commander was soon on his way to find better weapons.

There was some confusion regarding the numbering of the new regiments. The old law stated that there were to be twenty volunteer regiments, numbered one through twenty, and serving for twelve months. The new law, passed in May 1861, stated that there were also to be ten regiments of state troops, numbered one through ten, and mustered in to serve for three years or the duration of the war. To clear up the problem of having one regiment designated the 2nd North Carolina Volunteers and another regiment designated the 2nd North Carolina State Troops, the designation was changed on the volunteer regiments. Hence, the 2nd North Carolina Volunteers eventually became the 12th North Carolina State Troops.

John F. Hoke, adjutant general of North Carolina, authorized the formation of the 1st Regiment of Volunteers on April 29, 1861. Some of the companies were some of the oldest militia organizations in the state, like Company H, the Fayetteville Independent Blues, originally organized on August 23, 1793. Most Confederate infantry regiments only had ten companies. The 1st Volunteers had twelve, hailing from Edgecombe, Mecklenburg, Orange, Buncombe, Burke, Cumberland, Halifax, Lincoln, Bertie and Chowan Counties. The regiment was mustered into service on May 16, with West Point graduates Daniel H. Hill as colonel and Charles C. Lee as lieutenant colonel. Virginia Military Institute graduate James H. Lane was elected major. All three men had been teaching at the North Carolina Military Institute in Charlotte at the start of the war. On May 18, before North Carolina had officially left the Union, Governor Ellis had telegraphed the Confederate secretary of war offering him four regiments. The 1st Volunteers were on their way to Virginia on May 18 and on June 10 were fighting at Bethel Church. By the end of August 1861, North Carolina had organized and mustered into service sixteen infantry and cavalry regiments. These men came from the farms, cities and towns in the east and central portions of the state, as well as the coves and mountains in the west.

Tragedy struck just as North Carolina entered the fray. Governor John Ellis, who was in declining health, journeyed to Red Sulphur Springs in Virginia in an effort to regain his strength. Ellis died on July 7, 1861, at the age of forty-one. Since North Carolina had no lieutenant governor, Speaker of the Senate Henry T. Clark assumed the duties of governor. The 6th North Carolina State Troops served as an escort for Ellis's Raleigh funeral before dashing off to the war in Virginia.

On the Homefront: 1861

North Carolina was doing more than just organizing troops and sending them to Virginia: the coast of North Carolina was being fortified to withstand assault. Existing fortifications, like those at Forts Caswell and Macon, were being strengthened and guns mounted, while new works were being created. What would become Fort Fisher, the largest seacoast fortification in the Confederacy, was erected below Wilmington to protect blockade runners entering the Cape Fear River. On the Outer Banks, several earthen fortifications were constructed, including Fort Oregon at Oregon Inlet, Fort Ocracoke at Portsmith and Forts Clark and Hatteras at Hatteras Inlet. Coinciding with the fortifications, North Carolina purchased several small vessels that became known as the "Mosquito Fleet." The vessels were all armed with cannon and plied the waters outside the Outer Banks, capturing Northern merchant vessels. The *Winslow* captured the brig *Lydia Frances* the week of May 26, bound from Cuba to New York with a cargo of sugar. In a six-week period, the *Winslow* captured sixteen prizes. On July 10, the USS *Harriet Lane* arrived off Forts Clark and Hatteras and fired three salvos at the structures. For the first time, hostile shots had been fired in North Carolina. Northern merchants pressured the Federal government into launching a joint army-navy campaign, and Fort Clark fell on August 27 and Fort Hatteras surrendered on August 28. A short time later, Forts Ocracoke and Oregon were abandoned. This combined operation, which closed Pamlico Sound, boosted Northern morale, low since the Federal loss at Manassas in July.

The Confederates and Federals eyed one another nervously from their respective positions. The Federals, fearing a Confederate buildup on Roanoke Island, moved a regiment to the northern end of the island, near the village of Chicamacomico. The Confederates sensed an opportunity and captured a Federal ship worth an estimated $100,000 while landing supplies at Chicamacomico. The Confederates landed an infantry regiment and chased the Federals down the beach. A second Confederate force sent to cut off the Federals became grounded well off the coast. The following day, October 6, Federal reinforcements arrived, and the Confederates were forced to retreat. Newspapers christened the affair the Chicamacomico Races.

One final event was left to play out in North Carolina before the end of the year. There were several efforts during the war to install provisional governors of different Southern states to help bring those states back into the Union. The first in North Carolina occurred in November. Believing that much of eastern North Carolina was Unionist in its sentiments, a convention was held in Hatteras. Marble Nash Taylor, a Methodist minister, was elected governor of North Carolina by a handful of people. The convention repealed the secession ordinance and issued a call for congressional elections, with Hatteras as the new state capital. Later, Charles Foster was elected to Congress. Foster, a native of Maine, was a newspaper editor in Murfreesboro before locals expelled him for his Unionist sentiments. Foster was never seated by Congress, and Taylor soon disappeared. The Richmond *Daily Dispatch* considered Taylor "one of the most despicable of the human family—hated alike by God and man, and for the reason that he employs the garb of religion to cover the rottenness of his depraved and corrupt heart."

As 1861 ended, North Carolina had furnished more than forty regiments for Confederate service, created the Mosquito Fleet and disrupted shipping, lost a portion of the Outer Banks and had the ordinance of secession repealed by a sham government. And it was only the beginning of a long, bloody war.

Chapter 2

On the Homefront
1862

L ong considered the "Rip Van Winkle" state, North Carolina quickly "woke up" and became not only a large supplier of men to the Confederacy but also of war materials. North Carolina made cloth, uniforms, shirts, drawers and blankets, along with weapons and medical supplies.

In the state capital, Adjutant General James G. Martin established a clothing facility that provided forty-nine thousand jackets and sixty-nine thousand pair of pants, along with blankets and overcoats, during the first year of production. There was also in Raleigh a facility to manufacture bayonets, gunpowder, stationery, wooden shoes and school textbooks.

Several facilities in the state turned to producing weapons. After the capture of Harpers Ferry, Virginia, part of the machinery was shipped to Fayetteville, where rifles were produced for the Confederacy. Rifles were also produced in Asheville and Greensboro. Louis Froehlich manufactured swords in Wilmington under the name of the Wilmington Sword Company and later moved to Kenansville, operating as the Confederate States Arms Factory. In Wilmington, O.S. Baldwin made clothing, and Alfred A. Watson made flags.

Undoubtedly, Charlotte led the way in this war-driven industrial revolution. In January 1862, the North Carolina Powder Manufacturing Plant was established. A medical laboratory was established at the North Carolina Military Institute, collecting herbs and other resources to produce medicines. In 1862, the Confederate States Acid Works set up shop to manufacture fulminate of mercury that was used in percussion caps. The Rock Island Woolen Mills made uniforms; the new Manufacturing

Company of Charlotte made wooden canteens; A.M Taylor made metal canteens, mess pans and kettles; and J.M. Howie manufactured belt buckles. J.S. Phillips advertised that he "made to order" uniforms of "English grey clothes" and sold "Confederate staff buttons."

Many of the uniform manufacturers used a new workforce: women. The Charlotte facility alone employed three hundred. They would often do piecework, picking up material, taking it home and cutting it out and then returning the pieces to the factory to be sewn. Sometimes the uniforms were also sewn at home. The students at St. Mary's School in Raleigh recalled sewing uniforms and shirts and knitting socks and scarves.

Possibly the most important facility in the state was the Confederate Naval Yard in Charlotte. While not on the coast, the Queen City did have access to the coast via the railroad, and it had an established ironworks. After the fall of the Gosport Naval Yard in Norfolk, Virginia, in the spring of 1862, Confederate officials chose Charlotte as the primary naval yard. The facility included a gun carriage shop and a torpedo or mine shop and, with the help of the largest steam-powered hammer in the South, produced marine engines, solid shot, rifled shot, anchors and propeller shafts. The facility employed anywhere from 300 to 1,500 men at a time during the conflict, even though labor shortages toward the close of the war hurt production.

There were numerous iron mines across the state, able to supply much-needed iron ore to Confederate industries. They included the Bloomery Mine in Nash County, Costner Mine and Widow Bailey Place Mines in Lincoln County, Oremond Mine in Gaston County, Rodgers Mine in Stokes County, William Ore Bank in Yadkin County, Davidson River Iron Works in Henderson County and the Cranberry Iron Mines in Mitchell (now Avery) County. Work in the iron mines was done by hand, and then the ore was transported to the closest railroad. At Cranberry, there were forty men who worked at the mines throughout the war. Once the iron ore was loaded in a wagon, it was taken by a slave down the mountain to where the railroad ended east of Morganton, about forty-five miles. The iron ore was then loaded onto the train and transported to different points and various war purposes.

One highly prized necessity produced in North Carolina during the war was salt. Used to preserve food before the advent of refrigeration, salt was an essential commodity. There were not any salt mines in North Carolina, but many enterprising individuals along the coast took to producing salt during the war. Often, they took large kettles, or sometimes half of a locomotive boiler, and filled them full of seawater. Then fires were built underneath

To deal with the salt crisis in North Carolina, the state established salt works in Morehead City and later in Wilmington. *North Carolina State Archives*.

to boil away the water, leaving the salt. Since these operations were along the coast, the smoke from the fires was visible in the daytime, and the fires were kept burning twenty-four hours a day. Salt-producing facilities dotted the coast in places like Currituck Sound, New Topsail Inlet, Little River Inlet, Masonboro and Lockwood's Folly Inlet. The state set up its own salt commission with John M. Worth and, later, D.G. Worth, commissioners, while at the same time establishing a state salt works in Morehead City. When the state works were captured by the Federals, new works were established in Wilmington.

A plan was soon developed by the Federals to capture even more North Carolina property, further tightening the Federal blockade. The Confederates had built a series of forts on Roanoke Island and then obstructed the Croatan Sound to the west of the Island. Roanoke Island was twelve miles long and three miles wide, with one road that ran north–south. The largest amphibious expedition to date was launched on January 9. It took the better part of a month to sail the short distance from Maryland to North Carolina and get inside the bar at the Outer Banks. On the island, in a series of breastworks and sand and sod forts, the Confederates could muster a mere 1,400 soldiers, only a portion of which could be on line at a certain time due to the nature of the land. The Confederate line ran across the island and was defended by the forts and a seemingly impassable swamp. On February 7, the Confederate artillery at Fort Bartow opened fire. The guns of this fort were the only ones able to bear upon the Federal flotilla coming from the south. Twice during the day, the Mosquito Fleet ventured below the obstructions in the Sound, trying to entice the Federal gunboats toward the guns in the other Confederate forts. But the Federals refused to take the bait. By midnight, 10,000 Federal soldiers, with artillery, were ensconced on the island. A 200-man Confederate detachment, themselves with artillery, watched from nearby but made no effort to engage the Federals, thus losing an opportunity to delay the disembarkation of the Federal force. The Federals attacked along the only road on the morning of February 8, and the Confederate center was able to hold. Two Federal regiments were sent to the right, into the "impenetrable" swamps, and were able to gain the rear of the Confederate position. A charge by a Federal Zouave regiment further routed the Confederate defenders, and the island was lost. By nine o'clock that evening, the island was under Federal control. Confederate losses amounted to 23 killed, 58 wounded and 2,500 captured. Only a few Confederates were able to board small craft and sail away.

As the Federals under Major General Ambrose Burnside gained control of Roanoke Island, the Mosquito Fleet steamed up the Pasquotank River toward Elizabeth City. Once there, Commodore William F. Lynch looked over the situation and found only militia and a battery at Cobb's Point. The battery contained four guns, which Lynch considered a "wretchedly constructed affair," but only enough artillerists to man two of them. A Confederate gunboat was anchored nearby. A second gunboat, finding no ammunition to resupply, headed up the Dismal Swamp Canal for Norfolk. Early on the morning of February 10, the Federal gunboats steamed into

Elizabeth City was an important port town long before the war disrupted daily life. *From Harper's Weekly.*

view and charged straight at the Confederate ships. The militia fled, the Cobb's Point battery was lost and in about an hour's time, the Mosquito Fleet was destroyed. A second ship tried to run up the canal but, once the crew discovered that the hull was two inches too large to pass through the canal, it was scuttled and burned. Elizabeth City was evacuated, and at the urging of local Secessionists, the courthouse, two city blocks and a few other houses were burned. The fort was blown up, and the machine shops and railroad tracks were destroyed. On February 12, the Federals landed but stayed only a few hours.

Ten days later, several Federal gunboats sailed up the Chowan River toward the village of Winton. Word reached the Federal commander that the town harbored five hundred Unionists, plus it was set comparatively close to two railroads. Several hundred Confederate soldiers laid an ambush for the Federals, hiding in the underbrush along the bluffs of the river. A mulatto woman was stationed on the wharf to wave in the Federals. Just ten feet from the wharf, the Confederates were spotted by an officer on the gunboat. The Confederates opened fire with small arms and artillery, peppering the gunboat. After veering off to a safe distance, the Federals opened fire, outgunning the Confederate artillery and forcing the Confederates to retreat. After retiring a safe distance down the river, the Federals dropped anchor for the night. The next morning, they returned in force, shelling the riverbanks as they came. Once in Winton, they discovered that the Confederates had gone. They ransacked the town and then torched the buildings, the first time a civilian town was burned by the Federal army during the war.

That same day, February 20, Confederate prisoners captured at Roanoke Island were paroled and released at Elizabeth City. When a prisoner of war was paroled, he often went home to await orders to rejoin his regiment, promising not to take up arms until exchanged. Once a certain number of enemy soldiers were captured, the prisoners were exchanged, usually on paper. Thus, each former prisoner of war was considered free to rejoin his regiment.

Just a couple of weeks later, the Federal invasion force was again on the move. On March 11, a force containing both naval power and 11,000 infantry set out for New Bern. The Confederates, about 4,000 men under Brigadier General Lawrence Branch, were in a line of works about six miles below the city. The Confederate left was anchored by Fort Thompson. A line then ran one mile west toward the Atlantic and North Carolina Railroad. However, Branch did not have enough men to either finish the works or to carry them on to the swamp on the Confederate right. Like the

Some of the battle of New Bern was fought hand-to-hand. *From* Harper's Weekly.

Confederates near Elizabeth City, Branch was forced to call upon the militia, who took a position in the front line with regular, albeit untested, infantry and artillery soldiers. Even with the additional troops, there were large gaps in the Confederate line. Federal infantry disembarked near Slocum Creek on March 12 and soon started moving north through the rain. That evening, they bivouacked not far from the Confederate works. By 7:00 a.m. on March 13, the Federal attack force was on its way. The Federal troops struck the Confederate left first but were unable to penetrate the line of earthworks. On the Confederate center, the militia soon fled at the approach of the Federals, creating a gap in the line. Branch was able to plug the gap for a time, but Federal reinforcements exploited the breach, and the Confederate line collapsed, retreating back through New Bern. Only the burning of the bridge across the Trent River stopped the pursuing Federals, while the Confederates retreated to Kinston. For the Confederates, 578 were killed, wounded and captured, with 370 Federals reported as casualties. For many Confederate regiments, like the 26th North Carolina Troops under Colonel Zebulon Vance and the 37th North Carolina Troops under Colonel Charles C. Lee, New Bern was their first taste of battle. Dr. John B. Alexander of the 37th Regiment, a Charlotte native, wrote after the battle, "No man knows what a battle is until he is in one." For the regiments involved at New Bern, the list of battles would eventually be a long one.

The Federals were not quite finished with their campaign. April 18, 1862, found about three thousand Federal infantry sailing toward South Mills. Their goal was to destroy the lower locks on Dismal Swamp Canal, thus preventing Confederate ironclads from reaching Albemarle Sound and the

Slaves coming into New Bern following the battle. *From* Harper's Weekly.

Federal fleet. On April 18, a portion of the Federals disembarked at Chantilly in Camden County and began moving northwest. A Federal regiment sent ahead on April 19 was led astray by a local African American guide, whom they later shot, and lost the element of surprise. Confederate forces, about four hundred men with artillery, successfully defended their position for five hours before running low on ammunition. The Confederates redeployed closer to South Mills, but the Federals, fearing Confederate reinforcements, returned to their boats. The small battle, a tactical Confederate success, was welcome news.

About the same time that the Federals were trying to cut the Dismal Swamp Canal, another force was preparing to lay siege to Fort Macon, the last important Confederate coastal position between Norfolk, Virginia, to the north and Wilmington to the south. The Federals secured a beachhead on Bogue Banks on March 29 and commenced to transfer infantry and heavy, or siege, artillery. There were numerous skirmishes between Federal and Confederate infantry for the next three weeks. Twice, Federals gave fort commander Lieutenant Colonel Moses J. White a chance to surrender, and twice White refused. At 5:50 a.m. on April 25, the Federal land forces opened fire with mortars and large cannons, and the Federal ships offshore joined in at 8:40 p.m. The ships only fired for an hour; rough seas and a

Fort Macon, near Morehead City, was forced into submission by a joint army-navy bombardment. *From* Harper's Weekly.

few well-placed shots drove them out of the fort's range. With several guns dismounted by Federal artillery fire, and a large crack in the fort's walls near the powder magazine, the fort's commander hoisted a surrender flag. When White asked about terms, he was informed that the surrender would be unconditional, so White refused. The sides then agreed to meet again the next morning, when White was given new terms: the officers and men would be released on parole and were allowed to keep their personal effects. White agreed and signed the surrender terms after breakfast on the morning of April 26. Federal soldiers marched into Fort Macon, and Confederate prisoners of war were soon on their way to Beaufort or Fort Caswell. The Federals now had a port equal to that of Port Royal in South Carolina, used as a base for elements of the North Atlantic Blockading Squadron.

Only one week passed after the attack on Fort Sumter before Abraham Lincoln issued a blockade of Southern ports. The original proclamation did not include North Carolina, but as soon as the Tar Heel State became a de facto member of the Confederacy, the blockade was also ordered for the state's ports. The blockade covered 3,549 miles of coastline throughout the South and was the largest blockade ever undertaken by any nation. At first, the United States lacked crucial resources, like ships, to make the blockade effective. But as time passed, more ships were acquired, and other Southern ports were closed. May 1861 found only two Federal ships along North Carolina's coast, and it was not until June 1861 that the USS *Daylight* assumed position off the Cape Fear River, possibly the first blockade ship to do so. Supplies were needed by both the civilian population and the military, and individuals could stand to make a fortune by trying to run the blockade with needed supplies or with cotton to sell. Most of the blockaders entering Southern ports came via Nassau and the Bahamas, both owned by the British. Supplies from around the world were brought into these ports and often unloaded on smaller, steam-powered vessels. The vessels would then work their way up the coast, staying as close inland as possible, trying to blend into the wooded coastline. Usually, at night when there was no moon, the ships would attempt to steam past the Federal blockaders and into port. The unloading of cargo and the reloading often took as little as five days.

The Official Records of the United States Navy are full of reports of ships chased and seized along the North Carolina coast. The schooner *San Juan* was seized by the USS *Susquehanna* off Hatteras Inlet in September 1861, loaded with a cargo of salt, sugar and gin. The USS *Penobscot* captured the *Lizzie* off New Inlet on August 2, 1862, carrying a load composed of 220 sacks of salt, 1 bale of blankets, 5 boxes of tin, 2 cases of caustic soda, 2 tierces of soda ash, 1 case of enameled cloth and 2 boxes of arrowroot. In October 1862, the USS *Penobscot* captured the full-rigged brig *Robert Bruce* near Shallotte Inlet close to Cape Fear. It was loaded with 37 bales and 14 cases of woolens, 4 bales of linens, 26 cases of boots and shoes, 20 barrels of drugs, another 15 cases of drugs, 400 bundles of iron hoops, 225 pigs of iron and a number of bottles of ale, porter and rum, along with cutlery, earthenware, tinware, glue and corks.

A blockade runner stood a good chance of running the blockade. Between August 1, 1863, and September 29, 1864, 50 blockade runners were reported captured, but between May 20, 1863, and December 31, 1864, 260 ships entered the port of Wilmington with their cargoes. Some of the ships that docked in Wilmington were carrying luxury goods that brought inflated prices. Other ships were carrying military stores. The *Cornubia* ran the blockade and docked in August 1863. Its cargo included 228 cases of rifles from Austria, 459 cases of Austrian and British rifle ammunition, 52 bales of cartridge paper and 200 boxes of musket cartridges. The Cape Fear River emptied into the Atlantic Ocean at two different locations below Wilmington—the Old Inlet and the New Inlet. This caused the Federal navy to keep ships at both points, neither of which could easily support the other. Plus, with the numerous fortifications on Oak Island, Smith Island and below Wilmington, Federal ships had to keep a wide berth.

North Carolina chose to purchase its own blockade runner. Adjutant General James G. Martin suggested to Governor Clark that the state purchase a ship to bring much-needed materials from England. While Clark did not finish this task before his term of office expired, the next governor did. Cotton bonds in the neighborhood of $1,500,000 were issued, and John White and Thomas Crossan soon left for England to purchase not only a ship but shoes and blankets as well. The vessel they purchased was an iron-hulled side-wheeler named *Lord Clyde*. On June 28, 1863, the ship ran the blockade into Wilmington. The *Lord Clyde*'s registry was then changed, and the ship was renamed the *Advance*. In time, the *Advance* became the war's most successful blockade runner.

Shortages brought about by the closure of North Carolina ports, and the ensuing high prices, were a serious concern. However, an even greater threat to Confederate independence and the idea of state sovereignty appeared in the spring of 1862. The war was not going well for the Confederacy. Not only had much of the coast of North Carolina been closed by joint army-navy ventures, but other key sites were captured. Forts Henry and Donelson on the Tennessee River had fallen, opening Tennessee to Federal control. Port Royal, South Carolina, fell in November 1861, the port of Savannah, Georgia, was closed on April 11, 1862, and New Orleans fell on April 25. Added to this was the fact that the terms of men who had volunteered to serve in the army for just twelve months would soon finish, leaving the Confederate army in dire circumstances.

December 1861 brought serious talk in the Confederate Congress of a conscription act. The congressmen initially settled on a Furlough and Bounty Act that granted all twelve-month men a fifty-dollar bounty and a sixty-day furlough if they would reenlist. This maneuver failed to reap serious benefits, and on March 28, 1862, Jefferson Davis submitted to Congress a bill requiring all white, able-bodied men between the ages of eighteen and thirty-five to serve in the military for three years, or the duration of the war. The act passed on April 16 but exempted teachers, ministers, state employees, industrial workers and men who owned more than twenty slaves. The law also prevented one-year volunteers from leaving the army and authorized state militia officers to enforce the law. To help manage the system in North Carolina, Captain Peter Mallett, a son of a former North Carolina governor, was appointed supervisor in the state and promoted to major. Most of the volunteer training camps in North Carolina were closed, leaving the two principal camps located at Raleigh and Statesville. The law stipulated that regiments in the process of being formed had until May 17 to complete their organization. This date was later pushed back to July 8 and then August 1 to give men with lukewarm sentiments a chance to enlist of their own accord. Men voluntarily enlisting still had the right to go into companies of their own choosing and elect their own officers. Those who were conscripted could be assigned to any regiment. Conscription fell hardest on the yeoman farmers of North Carolina, and right when spring planting was taking place. Many farms that had already contributed a father or sons were now left with just women, children and the elderly.

No other act by the Confederate government was as despised as the conscription law. The *Fayetteville Observer* came out in favor of the act, informing its readers that it was not the right time to begin fighting over "rights and privileges. If we do not beat these Yankees, we shall soon have not the vestige of a right, not the shadow of a privilege, left us." William Holden and his *Weekly Standard* in Raleigh believed that conscription was "an invasion of the rights of the States, and as an engine of military despotism" and that there was "no good reason for urging a levy *en mass* on the people; and it is both wicked and dangerous to attempt to *force* free men to do what they have been doing, and will do *voluntarily*." The people in the state and the soldiers in the army were just as conflicted over conscription.

Added to these woes were continued raids by the Federal army and navy in eastern North Carolina. In July 1862, portions of the 1st North Carolina Cavalry battled three Federal gunboats in the Roanoke River. At Rainbow Bluffs, two miles below Hamilton, the cavalrymen ambushed the lead Federal craft. The Tar Heels were forced to retreat when the Federal sailors opened with artillery, but the surprise attack showed considerable pluck. The 1st Cavalry's attack was not the only land force versus navy engagement. Early that year, the 34th North Carolina Troops, under Colonel Collett Leventhorpe, attacked Federal gunboats at Gardner's Creek, a tributary of the Roanoke River, with both sides disengaging soon thereafter.

Also there were problems of a more internal nature. The powder mill in the Raleigh area exploded in June 1862, killing four. And there were Unionist uprisings in the town of Washington and in Davidson County. At one point, Governor Clark ordered three hundred militiamen into Davidson County to suppress the dissidents. Many cities in the central portion of the state, like Raleigh and Fayetteville, had to deal with refugees from the eastern counties overrun by the Federals. W.W. Fife, a merchant in New Bern, fled the coastal cities when the Federals arrived, moving his family to Thomasville in Davidson County and opening a new general merchandise store.

In the midst of the confusion, North Carolina men went to the polls to elect a new governor. Governor Ellis had died in July 1861 and was replaced by Henry Clark, the president of the Senate. There were two principal parties in North Carolina: Democrats, also known as the

Confederate Party, and the Conservative Party. The Confederate Party considered success by the Southern military critical for independence and wholeheartedly supported Jefferson Davis's policies. Democrats were also willing to suppress their convictions regarding states' rights for the greater Confederate cause. Many of the Conservatives were originally Unionists who were opposed to secession until Lincoln's call for troops; they were strong supporters of states' rights and frequently opposed the Confederate government when it infringed on those rights. The Confederate Party advanced William J. Johnston of Charlotte, a member of the secession convention and president of the Charlotte and South Carolina Railroad. The Conservatives nominated Zebulon B. Vance, a Buncombe County native, former congressional representative and colonel of the 26th North Carolina Troops. Neither candidate canvassed the state, partially due to the fact that Vance was stationed in Virginia. The parties heavily relied on their supporting newspapers to advance their platforms, with eleven newspapers backing Johnston and ten backing Vance. The Confederate Party promoted the image of being "more loyal and more fully committed to Confederate Independence" and believed the war should go on until "the last extremity"

Edward Stanly, former North Carolina congressman, was appointed military governor by Abraham Lincoln in 1862. *North Carolina State Archives.*

with "no compromise with enemies, traitors, and tories." The Conservatives believed that the war should go on but insisted that civil liberties should be protected at all hazards. On principle, they were opposed to the conscription act. In the end, Vance won by a landslide, capturing 72 percent of the total vote and sixty-eight of eighty counties. Vance, just thirty-two years old, assumed office on September 8. Shortly thereafter, the Conservatives removed most of the Democrats from public office.

Surprisingly, Vance was not the only governor in North Carolina in 1862. In April, Abraham Lincoln appointed Tar Heel native Edward Stanly as provisional or military governor of North Carolina. Stanly was a five-term congressional delegate from North Carolina in the 1830s and 1840s before migrating to California, where he unsuccessfully ran for governor in 1857 on the Republican ticket. Stanly arrived in New Bern in May 1862, with the idea that North Carolina had been coerced out of the Union by a few individuals. Most believed that Stanly was a traitor, and his repeated attempts to meet with Vance went unheeded. In August 1862, Stanly was authorized by Lincoln to hold congressional elections in the parts of eastern North Carolina that were under Federal control. These elections happened on January 1, 1863, in four counties: Beaufort, Carteret, Craven and Hyde. Jennings Pigott, a native of Carteret County and prewar agent in Washington, D.C., was elected to represent that area in the United State Congress. The House Committee of Elections refused to seat Pigott because of voting irregularities and because Pigott was considered a sojourner in North Carolina, not a resident. Soon after the election, Stanly resigned as provisional governor, a sign of protest over Lincoln's Emancipation Proclamation. Daniel Reeves Goodloe, also a Tar Heel native and a leading abolitionist newspaper editor in Washington, D.C., was considered a replacement for Stanly, but Lincoln never acted on the appointment, and attempts to reconstruct North Carolina during the war came to an end.

Vance had more to contend with than Stanly. Prices were rising all across the state on the basic commodities that sustained life, the conscription acts were creating dissidents from the mountains to the sea and the Federals continued to occupy almost all of the eastern portions of the state. Federals in the east began to receive reinforcements in October 1862, and the Federal commander now felt strong enough to mount offensive operations against the important railroads that ran through the eastern part of the state.

About five thousand Federals, under the command of Major General John G. Foster, left Washington, North Carolina, on November 2 and headed west. Their goals were three Confederate regiments supposedly foraging in the area. The first skirmish took place late that afternoon at Little Creek, with the Confederates fighting a delaying action. A second skirmish took place toward dark at Rawl's Creek, with the Confederates retreating during the night. November 3 found the Federals passing through Williamston, where they liberated a number of chickens and sweet potatoes. The next afternoon, they pillaged and burned parts of the town of Hamilton. Fearing the concentration of Confederates in the area, the Federals turned toward Plymouth and were then transferred to New Bern by the navy. The navy set out on its own expedition on November 23. The USS *Ellis*, under the command of Lieutenant William B. Cushing, went to destroy the salt works on New Topsail Inlet and Jacksonville, taking possession of the latter and capturing two schooners loaded with $30,000 worth of cotton and turpentine. On November 24, while heading out, Cushing ran the *Ellis* aground. Despite all of the crew's efforts, the ship stuck fast. Everything save one of the two cannons was unloaded onto one of the captured ships, which sailed away. The following morning, the Confederate land batteries attacked, and for an hour or so, Cushing and six other men who had been selected to remain behind traded shots with four guns on the shore. Cushing then gave the order to abandon ship, setting the *Ellis* on fire.

Several companies of the 17th North Carolina, under Lieutenant Colonel John Lamb, with cavalry and a battery of artillery, captured Plymouth on November 10, driving the Federals from the town and river. The following day, ten thousand Federals under Foster set out from New Bern toward Goldsboro and the railroad bridge over the Neuse River. They found Confederates dug in on the opposite bank of Southwest Creek on November 13 but were able to flank the Confederates out of their position. The Confederates fell back to a strong position two miles from Kinston and entrenched. Foster attacked this position on the morning of December 14 and turned the Confederate left flank. Thinking all the Confederates had retreated to the far side of the bridge, the Confederate commander, Brigadier General Nathan Evans, ordered the bridge destroyed. He then ordered Confederate artillery to open fire on his former entrenchments, which he assumed were manned by the Federals. The remaining Confederates retreated in some order until they came in sight of the burning bridge, and then panic ensued. Many of the Confederates chose to scurry across the flaming bridge, but about four hundred were captured. The Confederates fell back two miles beyond Kinston and regrouped. Foster sent the Confederates a demand for surrender, to which Evans replied with, "Tell your General to go to h—l!" After ransacking Kinston, the Federals then

On the Homefront: 1862

Thomas Clingman was a prewar
United States senator and then
a Confederate brigadier general.
Library of Congress.

moved toward Goldsboro. On December 16, the Federals cut the telegraph lines and railroad at Mount Olive, attempted to destroy a gunboat being built in the Neuse River and fought a spirited, long-range engagement at White Hall. The following day, Foster moved the bulk of his command to Goldsboro and again clashed with Confederates, this time under Brigadier General Thomas Clingman. The bridge was burned, and a shot through the boiler damaged a locomotive pulling a load of reinforcements and an iron-plated car equipped with an artillery piece. The Federals then chose to return to New Bern, and the railroad was repaired in two weeks.

There was one final act for 1862. On December 31, while being towed by the USS *Rhode Island* from Hampton Roads to Beaufort, South Carolina, the famed USS *Monitor* was swamped by the heavy seas and sank off Cape Hatteras. Of the sixty-two seamen aboard, sixteen perished. The *Monitor* had dueled with the CSS *Virginia* in Hampton Roads in the spring of 1862 in an indecisive naval engagement, the first of its kind in the world. Now, the celebrated ship lay with so many others off the coast of North Carolina.

Chapter 3
On the Homefront
1863

For many North Carolinians, 1862 was a tough year. Battles fought in Virginia, Maryland and Tennessee found Tar Heels at the front, and many a Tar Heel native filled a soldier's grave or a bed at an improvised hospital. When it came to hospitals, North Carolina took a leading role soon after leaving the Union. By July 1861, the state had established a hospital in Raleigh, three in Virginia and wayside hospitals along the railroads in Weldon, Tarboro, Goldsboro, Raleigh, Salisbury and Charlotte. Many of these hospitals and wayside stations were dependent on local citizens for supplies. Some communities went ever further. In Charlotte, local ladies established the Hospital Association of Mecklenburg County, with Mrs. J.H. Wilson as president. Next, the group sent two young ladies, a Miss Gibbon and Mrs. Bolton, with five servants, to Yorktown, Virginia, to serve as nurses for Tar Heel soldiers. Shortly thereafter, the North Carolina Hospital in Petersburg, Virginia, gained the services of Mrs. Kennedy of Wilmington, Mrs. Beasley of Plymouth and Miss M.L. Pettigrew of Raleigh as nurses.

The Hospital Association of Mecklenburg County was just the first in a long line of relief groups organized during the war for the benefit of soldiers. Just about every county or large city had at least one organization trying to provide for the soldiers on the front lines. In August 1861, the Soldiers Aid Society of Wilmington was organized, taking donations and religious materials, blankets, shirts, drawers and socks. In Raleigh, there were at least five aid societies. The Baptist, Methodist and Episcopal Churches each organized one, and then there was the citywide Raleigh Sick

North Carolina established several hospitals in order to treat wounded soldiers, including the Pettigrew Hospital in Raleigh. *North Carolina Museum of History.*

Soldiers Relief Society, open to everyone. The fifth group was organized by the men of the city who were not in the army and was entitled the Raleigh Mutual Relief and Charitable Association. This group provided fuel, like wood, and food to the needy in the city. The ladies in Fayetteville formed the Cumberland County War Association, which provided assistance to families in need in the surrounding areas. This group was joined by the Young Ladies Knitting Society and the Juvenile Knitting Society, both in the Fayetteville area. In Orange County, the aid society met in the courthouse in Hillsboro every week, "sewing garments, knitting socks, furnishing food, looking after the sick, or wounded soldiers passing by." The Military Sewing Society in Washington was created on April 23, 1861, and made uniforms for local soldiers. Later, these ladies nursed some three hundred Georgia soldiers stationed in their community who were ill with typhoid fever and the measles. Even rural mountain communities formed aid societies. In Caldwell County, the Ladies of Lenoir provided shirts, pants, socks, haversacks, blankets, bandages and food, besides raising money: $166 in just two weeks in one instance. Many groups collected items from surrounding communities and forwarded them to individual companies.

At times, individuals tried to help family members in need. Watauga County native Leah Adams Doughtery recalled that as a little girl, she could be "call[ed] out of bed any hour of the night to cook and pack a knapsack with three-day[s'] rations." In other cases, churches became involved. Churches of all denominations in Hillsboro, Charlotte, Fayetteville, Edenton, Halifax, Pittsboro, Tarboro, Wilmington and Raleigh all sent bells, often to

Tredegar Iron Works in Richmond, Virginia, to be recast as cannons for the Confederacy. Some churches took up donations; Bethel Baptist Church in McDowell County, in July 1862, sent $15.15 to purchase "testaments and religious literature" for the 58th North Carolina Troops. Many of the state's religious newspapers sent tracts, Bibles and missionaries into the field. Each Confederate regiment had its own chaplains. In the spring of 1862, Reverend Alfred L. Stough, a member of the 37th North Carolina Troops, wrote the state Baptist paper, the *Biblical Reporter*, that his regiment had a strong religious interest but needed more Bibles and other "religious reading matter." He finished his letter with "Pray for us. Pray for our unfortunate nation, that we may have a speedy and honorable peace." The religious movement that Stough noted in his regiment was spreading throughout the entire army and, eventually, the state as well. Several churches experienced their own revivals during the war years.

January 1, 1863, brought about the official adoption of Abraham Lincoln's Emancipation Proclamation. The proclamation was to free all the enslaved people in all states "in rebellion against the United States." Areas under Union control, like Kentucky, Maryland, portions of Louisiana and the new slave state of West Virginia, were excluded. The proclamation failed its stated purpose—to free all enslaved people—largely due to the fact that the Federal army was not in control of those areas. However, the proclamation did change the purpose of the war for the North. Prior to January 1, the focus had been on the preservation of the Union. Now, Federal soldiers were fighting to enforce the proclamation. Many Northern Democrats were opposed to the proclamation, while there are stories of Federal officers resigning from the army or of enlisted men deserting, refusing to fight for the abolition of slavery. Of course, many across the South were also opposed. The editor of the *Fayetteville Observer* noted that the proclamation was not worth "the paper it was written on, except" that the document gave the South more reason to fight. The *Weekly Standard* in Raleigh considered the proclamation "Desperate Measures." In some areas, when word of Lincoln's act reached the slaves, they were apt to desert their masters. H.G. Spruill, mayor of Williamston in Martin County, wrote, "Nearly all of mine are all in town [Plymouth, and] keep out of my site." A Buncombe County native "was roused to a feeling of indignation inexpressible" on hearing of Lincoln's proclamation. "[I]t did more than anything else to alienate the affections of the common people." Governor Vance wrote after the war that that the proclamation opened "a wide door to demagogues to appeal to the non-slave holding class, and make them believe that the only issue was the protection of slavery, in which they were sacrifices for the sole benefit of the masters."

Changes to the Confederate command structure in Virginia in February 1863 brought changes to eastern North Carolina. In an effort to protect the crucial supply lines below Petersburg, the Confederate high command launched operations toward Suffolk in Virginia and New Bern and Washington in North Carolina. Major General Daniel H. Hill, first colonel of the 1st North Carolina Volunteers, took command, prompting the Raleigh *Progress* to write that Hill was "one of the best fighting men in the service." Hill chose first to move on New Bern with a three-pronged attack. On March 13, the first of those prongs struck the Federals about ten miles from the town, capturing two lines of works. A counterattack on March 14 by the Federals did not recapture the position, and the Federals retreated back to New Bern. An attack that same day on Fort Anderson at New Bern produced few positive results: the Union gunboats were able to drive off the attacking party before they could storm the fort. The third prong, tasked with damaging the railroad, also failed, and Hill was forced to withdraw his men from the vicinity of New Bern. Hill next turned his attention to Washington and, by March 30, had drawn up siege lines around the town. General Foster was in Washington directing the movements of the Federals. He had arranged for two different relief columns. The first, by water, took one look at the Confederate fortifications on the river and returned to New Bern. The second fought a skirmish at Blount's Creek on April 9 and retreated to New Bern. Foster realized that he needed to return to New Bern to lead the relief column himself and slipped through the Confederate blockade on April 15. The Confederates, having finished the objective of gathering much-needed food and supplies from the surrounding area, started leaving the Washington defenses about the same time. Soon thereafter, the Confederates in Virginia began a buildup for the second Northern invasion, and much of Hill's command rejoined the Army of Northern Virginia. The Federals made a demonstration against the railroad toward Kinston on May 22, and while they were at first successful, they were later driven back toward New Bern. June was relatively quiet.

Vance had other problems, even greater than unsuccessful Confederate attacks, Union raids and the Emancipation Proclamation. Unionism and dissension were overrunning North Carolina. The Unionist element in North Carolina had never really died down with the wave of Confederate enthusiasm that swept through the state with Lincoln's April 1861 call for volunteers to suppress the rebellion. Often, the two sides clashed. In May

1861, on the day of the election of delegates for the secession convention, the pro-Confederate sheriff of Madison County took a shot at a pro-Union voter, wounding the man's son instead. The sheriff rushed to a nearby house and locked himself in a second-story room. Standing on the balcony, he dared the "damned black Republicans" to open fire, and the father of the wounded boy obliged, wounding the sheriff. The town constable then stepped in and was attempting to arrest the sheriff when the father rushed in and fired a second time, killing the sheriff. Afterward, the father fled to Kentucky and joined the Union army. In June 1861, the Unionist element in Randolph County was supposedly organized, armed and ready to fight pro-Confederate neighbors. By August 1861, Governor Ellis ordered troops into the central part of the state—Randolph, Guilford, Davidson, Forsyth, Davie, Yadkin and Wilkes Counties—to suppress dissidents. A war of words and in the courts broke out in the town of Washington. Local Secessionists fought to keep local Unionists from prominent positions in the local militia. After losing the October 1861 militia officer elections in one district in the area, the Secessionists moved to invalidate the results. The Confederate authorities responded by dispatching cavalry into the area and arresting a leading Unionist, which led to a change of sentiments.

In January 1863, Vance asked the general assembly to make aiding and abetting deserters a crime, while at the same time issuing a pardon of clemency to absent-without-leave soldiers who voluntarily returned to their regiments. That same month, militia and regular Confederate soldiers, namely the 56th North Carolina Troops, began sweeping through counties that held large groups of deserters and those evading conscription. In many instances, the militia officers charged with carrying out Confederate conscription were ineffectual. They never had enough men to fulfill their duty and, at the same time, feared retaliation by family members of those they arrested. Numerous militia officers wrote Vance, complaining that their barns and other outbuildings were burned or pulled down in retaliation. Draft dodgers in Germantown, Stokes County, swore to "die at home rather than go" into Confederate service. Fifty mothers, wives and daughters from Iredell, Wilkes and Yadkin Counties implored Vance to return their conscripted husbands before they all starved. Confederate commanders in the central counties started holding horses of local dissidents hostage until the men turned themselves in, while at the same time, frequent letters arrived on Vance's desk about the abuses, robbery and assaults committed by Confederate soldiers.

Desertion plagued North Carolina regiments, especially after the conscription act of 1862. Men came home to plant and harvest crops, to

The home of Colonel Lawrence Allen of the 64th North Carolina Troops was visited in January 1863 during the salt raid. *Author's collection.*

take care of sick family members or simply because they felt they had done their duty. Montreville Ray signed up on May 1, 1861, to serve one year in the 16th North Carolina Troops. He deserted on May 1, 1862, coming back home to Yancey County. Officers and governmental officials tried everything possible to entice soldiers to return to their regiments, including several general amnesties. Yet soldiers continued to leave, by themselves or in groups. Between 12 and 15 men deserted from the 3rd North Carolina State Troops in August 1863. Several were killed and others captured by conscription bureau soldiers a few days after they left. The remaining prisoners were tried, returned to their regiments and executed on the grounds of Montpelier in Virginia. Desertions were extreme from the ranks of the 58th North Carolina Troops. While records are incomplete, there were at least 707 deserters from this regiment. General Johnston had 12 of its members, along with 2 from the 60th Regiment, executed on May 4, 1864, outside Dalton, Georgia. These executions seldom stopped desertion.

That same January, one of the most infamous acts of the war occurred in Madison County. Salt, when it could be had, was selling for large sums. Many counties had a salt agent who was responsible for distribution to loyal, or Confederate, families. The families in Shelton Laurel were not pro-Confederate.

On one cold January night, several men, perhaps as many as fifty, slipped into Madison and broke into the building where the salt was stored. They then raided a few homes, including that of Colonel Lawrence Allen of the 64th North Carolina Troops. Allen's children were sick with scarlet fever, and at least one account described the raiders taking the blankets off the beds of the children. Once word reached the camp of the 64th Regiment, of which large portions hailed from Madison County, the men asked to be sent back to the mountains to deal with the raiders. Some of the raiders were actually deserters from the 64th Regiment. Other contingents of Confederates were soon scouring the mountains. Portions of the 64th Regiment, marching into Madison County in two columns, converged on Shelton Laurel. In one skirmish, eight deserters and dissidents were killed. In another, fifty men took a stand against the 64th Regiment, losing six before being driven off. A group of twelve was captured and sent to the jail in Asheville. Many Shelton Laurel residents were tortured and flogged, and another fifteen were captured. Allen presently learned that one of his sick children had died, and the other was not expected to live. He arrived in Marshall in time to have his daughter die in his arms. Fifteen Shelton Laurel men and boys were told that they were going to be taken to Knoxville and tried. Instead, thirteen of them were taken a little way up the road and, in groups of five, executed. The oldest was sixty, the youngest thirteen. Vance was furious and ordered an investigation, but the Confederate high command took little notice.

While the affair in Madison County was horrific, a confrontation in Yadkin County had even greater statewide ramifications. In February 1863, a dozen Yadkin County militiamen came upon a group of sixteen bushwhackers in a schoolhouse near Yadkinville. In a brief exchange of gunfire, two men on each side were killed before some of the bushwhackers escaped into the surrounding woods. Three were caught and requested writs of habeas corpus from the North Carolina Supreme Court. Judge Richmond Pearson ordered the bushwhackers released, ruling that the militia had no legal authority to enforce a national law. Since there was no Confederate supreme court to which one could appeal, the states remained in limbo regarding the enforcement of the Conscription Act. For a short time, Governor Vance retracted his orders to the militia, instead asking them to assist Confederate officers in the execution of the Conscription Act. But the rise in desertions became so great that Vance again had to order the militia to round up those absent without leave.

On the heels of conscription came another highly controversial congressional act. In April 1863, the Confederate Congress passed its first comprehensive tax laws. One section of the new tax code required certain professional men to pay a fee for a license. Tobacconists, livery stable keepers, cattle brokers, butchers, bakers, apothecaries, photographers, lawyers, physicians and confectioners all had to pay $50. Bankers were required to pay $500. Another part of the tax code was referred to as tax-in-kind. Farmers, after keeping a certain percentage for their own consumption, were assessed with a debt of one-tenth of their agricultural production. Local agents, who were despised, collected wheat, oats, corn, rice, potatoes, fodder, sugar, cotton, wool, tobacco and rye. These items were then sent to local, and then regional, collection points to be forwarded to the army. The program was highly unpopular, and many citizens gathered frequently to denounce the measure, along with other threats to state sovereignty and personal freedoms. For many of the lower and lower-middle classes of people in North Carolina, it was the first time they had been required to pay a tax, and for many in this demographic who practiced only subsistence farming, the program literally took food from needy families. In the end, the people in North Carolina contributed more than any other state to the loathed form of taxation.

The plight of the pro-Confederate people, the problems caused by Judge Pearson and the Conscription Act and the peace movement that was afoot led Vance and the General Assembly to create the Guard for Home Defense in July 1863. All able-bodied white men between the ages of eighteen and fifty, including those who were exempt from Confederate service, like militia officers, comprised the Home Guard. The new organization was specifically charged with arresting deserters and draft dodgers and protecting pro-Confederate families. The deserters and draft dodgers went by different names in different parts of the state. In the east, they were known as "buffaloes," in the central counties "outliers" and in the western sections "bushwhackers" or "Tories." These men could be deserters from either army, those who sought to evade military service or those who simply preferred the life of a robber or highwayman. At the same time, a new law enacted by the General Assembly fined those aiding and abetting deserters up to $500, with possible imprisonment. As it was for the militia system, the state was divided up for home guard coverage. Many counties had one or two home guard companies, which usually rotated in and out of service, often for a week at a time. These companies or battalions were part of regiments. In the west, Vance commissioned Yancey County militia colonel John W. McElroy as commander of the 1st Brigade of North Carolina Home Guard. McElroy rotated his headquarters between Madison County, often on the campus of

Collett Leventhorpe served as colonel of the 11th North Carolina State Troops and, later, brigadier general of home guard forces. *Library of Congress.*

Mars Hill College, and Burnsville in neighboring Yancey County. Outside his militia experiences, McElroy had no military background. In the central and eastern parts of the state, Vance commissioned former colonel of the 11th North Carolina State Troops Collett Leventhorpe as brigadier general. Leventhorpe, a former officer in the British army, had ample experience.

In many instances, the home guard faced organized and well-equipped men with combat experience. There were rumors of a group in Mitchell County, near Roan Mountain, that numbered up to 200 men. Randolph County had an organized group of 31 men, and a group along the Chatham-Moore County line boasted "that they numbered now eleven hundred men." The Montgomery-Moore-Chatham-Randolph County area was so notorious as a deserter haven that "deserters from other states make their way thither and often stop along the road to enquire directions." In Wilkes County, a group, sometimes estimated at 1,100 men strong, "march[ed] under an old dirty United States rag!" In Wilkes County on August 30, 1863, a group of 300 Unionists marched into the county seat and, raising the flag of the United States, made speeches for the Union and for peace.

Realizing that he needed help, Vance contacted Robert E. Lee, who responded by sending the 21st and 56th Regiments and a squadron of cavalry, all under the command of Brigadier General Robert F. Hoke. The Tar Heel native stationed his forces in Wilkes and surrounding counties and commenced rounding up deserters. By mid-October, over five hundred had been captured and sent to prison, the conscript camp or back to their regiments. For a short amount of time, things were quiet in the central counties.

As Vance sought to control the Unionist and dissident elements in the central and western portions of the state, the Federal army continued to launch raids from its bases along the eastern seaboard. Brigadier General Edward Potter led Federal cavalry on a successful raid in July 1863, capturing Greenville and destroying $300,000 worth of property, including the Tar River bridge. A Federal battalion then struck Tarboro, burning a half-finished ironclad, railroad equipment, cotton and quartermaster goods. Rocky Mount was captured, and supply wagons, a flour mill, machine shop and more cotton were torched. The raiding column was back in New Bern by July 23. Three days later, Foster led five regiments from Winton toward Weldon. They were attacked by the home guard but were able to overwhelm the 200 men of the local force. On July 28, 250 Federal cavalrymen almost captured Confederate general Matt Ransom, who was out scouting. Ransom raced back to find his men bathing at Boone's Mill. Some of the men, though naked, fought the Federals, while others removed the planking from the bridge. After several hours of skirmishing, the Federals retreated, believing that they were facing a superior force, and the railroad bridge at Weldon was saved.

Summer and fall brought numerous confrontations to the eastern and western portions of North Carolina. In the east, there were minor skirmishes in Washington, Edenton, Pasquotank, Ford's Mill and Hertford. Numerous blockade runners were captured, including the *Robert E. Lee* off Cape Fear, the *Banshee* off Cape Lookout and the *Margaret and Jesse*, also off Cape Lookout. In the west, the Federals took firm control of east Tennessee in September 1863, and the Great Smoky Mountains became the barrier separating the two sides. However, there were numerous passes through the mountains, and raids became frequent, like the two hundred to three hundred Federals who occupied Waynesville in mid-September. In mid-October, local Confederates skirmished with local Unionists near Murphy. The Confederates followed the ringleader, Goldman Bryson, back to his home and killed him.

With Federal ships cruising the sea, Federal soldiers occupying much of the East Coast, Federals perched just to the east in Tennessee and the rise of Unionism and dissidents, it would be hard to imagine any more woe for Vance and other state officials to handle. Yet in mid-1863, another faction

Zebulon Baird Vance was colonel of the 26th North Carolina Troops and, from 1862 to 1865, governor of North Carolina. *North Carolina Museum of History*.

rose up to confront the leaders of North Carolina. Following the dreadful Federal losses at Fredericksburg and Chancellorsville, the Democratic Party in the North began clamoring for peace. With the dual Southern defeats at Gettysburg and Vicksburg, some North Carolinians began to trot out the rallying cry of the Democrats: "The Constitution as it is, the Union as it was." Leading the charge was newspaper editor William W. Holden, who, beginning in June 1863, began to call for peace through the columns of the *North Carolina Standard*. Holden believed that the only solution "to arrest this awful evil" was to demand peace. But that peace had to "preserve the rights of the sovereign States and the institutions of the South." Holden believed that the "two governments are so inflamed by the war spirit, and so intent on mere physical triumphs, that unless the people of the two sections rise up and demand…to close the war…the war may be prolonged indefinitely."

Holden's words caught like fire. Between July 3 and September 9, 1863, there were close to one hundred peace rallies held in North Carolina. While a few of these were held in the eastern and western sections of the state, the vast majority, almost 80 percent, took place in the central North Carolina counties. Holden publicized many of these gatherings and encouraged others to speak out. At many of these meetings, resolutions were adopted, like those from the meeting in Surry County, which stated: "That in our opinion, under the circumstances, the best thing the people of North Carolina could do would be to go for the 'Constitution as it is, and the Union as it was.'" The meetings grew as the summer continued. In Stanley County, 600 to 700 people gathered, with 1,200 to 1,500 at a peace meeting in Forsyth County.

The peace movement, with all of its rhetoric, split the Conservative Party in September 1863. There was the Peace wing of the Conservative Party and the War wing. Often these two sides clashed, both in the press and, at times, physically. At a Cabarrus County meeting in August 1863, the two sides sparred, with several broken bones the result. Vance believed that Holden "is for submission, reconstruction or any thing else that will put him back under Lincoln and stop the war." On September 9, Vance was at home in Raleigh when he was informed that Georgia soldiers were wrecking the office of Holden's *North Carolina Standard*. Grabbing an officer from a local hotel, Vance went to the business and persuaded the troops that freedom of speech and the press was "purchased by the richest blood of their patriotic fathers." The troops dispersed, and Vance returned home to find Holden seeking asylum. Early the next morning, Vance was again called out. This time a group of Holden supporters was ransacking the office of the Secessionist *State Journal*. Vance, with Holden at his side, quieted this crowd and sent them home. A third riot took place later that day, this time led by Alabama troops passing through town. Once again Vance rode to the scene and quieted the crowd, afterward complaining to Jefferson Davis. The president later ordered that all troops passing through the city to Virginia could not disembark, and order returned. The peace movement drew many of the Unionists into their ranks, while the old Confederate party allied with the war Conservatives.

Peace meetings were held not only in North Carolina but throughout the South. Riots were not confined to Raleigh. Women, upset over inflation and the inability to purchase food for their families, led bread riots in Atlanta, Georgia, on March 17 and Salisbury, North Carolina, a day later. A women-led riot took place in Richmond, Virginia, followed by six others before 1863 ended. A group of women from Bladen County, calling themselves "Regulators," told Vance in a letter a week before the Salisbury riot that "the time has come that we the common people has to hav bread or blood and we are bound boath men and women to hav it or die in the attempt." According to the *Carolina Watchman*, on Wednesday morning, March 18, forty to fifty women, mostly wives of soldiers, asked a Salisbury merchant to sell them goods at non-inflated prices. When the merchant refused, the women began to take hatchets to the door of the shop. The merchant soon gave the flour to the ladies. The women struck other establishments and were given other food stores before returning home.

The peace meeting, splintering of the Conservative Party, riots, the creation of the home guard, blockade, Federal raids and inflation all showed that the great Confederacy was breaking apart. And the worst was yet to come.

Chapter 4

On the Homefront
1864

C ampaign after campaign, with a seemingly endless series of battles, made headlines through 1864. News stories abounded of the Overland Campaign in Virginia, with the battles at the Wilderness, Spotsylvania Court House, North Anna Church and Cold Harbor in the east; and the north Georgia campaign, with battles at Dalton, Resaca, Pickett's Mill, Kolb's Farm and Kennesaw. But campaigns and raids were also ostensibly commonplace in the Tar Heel State.

Just two days into the new year, Robert E. Lee decided that he could spare men for a campaign in eastern North Carolina, and Major General George E. Pickett was sent south with thirteen thousand soldiers. The expedition against New Bern was launched on January 30, and while the overall campaign was a failure and led to Pickett's removal, the campaign did have some highlights. The men under Brigadier General Robert F. Hoke accomplished the task of capturing the Federals along Batchelder's Creek. While the second column captured some outer defensive works, they, along with the third column, were unable to mount an attack. The sailors on the Neuse River did manage to capture the USS *Underwriter*, stationed near Fort Anderson and New Bern, in a daring raid in which they boarded the ship and fought hand-to-hand with the Federal naval "jacks." Also, a divisionary movement out of Wilmington toward Morehead City led by Brigadier General James G. Martin took Newport Barracks, completely routing the Federals. At the end, the Confederates were forced to withdraw. As an aside, one event nearly cost Pickett his life after the war. Pickett found

Brigadier General James G. Martin served in various posts in North Carolina during the war. In 1865, he was commanding the Department of Western North Carolina. *Library of Congress.*

that among his prisoners were several former members of the 66th North Carolina Troops, who had deserted and joined the Union army. After a trial in Kinston, twenty-two of them were convicted and hanged in groups through February; resentment over Pickett's actions continued to fester long after the war.

Pickett was soon recalled to Virginia, and his second-in-command, Robert Hoke, took over the expedition. Hoke turned his attention on the coastal town of Plymouth, planning a joint army-navy mission. To help with the navy side, Hoke recruited the almost-complete iron *Albemarle* to join in the attack. The *Albemarle* was one of three 150-foot-long, iron-plated river gunboats built in North Carolina, the others being the *Neuse* and an unnamed and unfinished ship under construction on the Tar River. The *Albemarle* was constructed in a cornfield on the Roanoke River, mostly of re-rolled railroad iron. The ship had sloping sides, which deflected enemy shot, and two 6.4-inch Brooke rifled cannons, one forward and the other aft, and each capable of firing from three different fixed-gun ports. The ship also contained a ram and was powered by two three-bladed screw propellers connected to two two-hundred-horsepower steam engines. The plan was for Commander James W. Cooke to sail down the river and support Hoke's attack on Plymouth.

Hoke's attacking force, composed mostly of North Carolinians, was on the outskirts of Plymouth on April 17, 1864. Artillery was freely used by both sides. At one point, Confederate artillery struck the USS *Bombshell*, which was attempting to help the Federal forts and received several shots below the waterline. The ship limped back to Plymouth, was tied up at the wharf and promptly sank. On the afternoon of April 18, Matt Ransom's brigade made a demonstration against one portion of the Federal lines while Hoke's brigade, under Colonel John T. Mercer, charged another portion of the Federal line. While it took several attempts to charge the works, the Federals eventually gave way, and the Confederates took a portion of the fortifications. Mercer was killed in the assault. The *Albemarle* joined the attack on April 20, sinking the USS *Southfield*. The *Albemarle* rammed the *Southfield*, and as the *Southfield* began to sink, the *Albemarle* was unable to pull away. Finally, the *Southfield* hit the bottom of the river and turned on its side, and the *Albemarle* was able to free itself. Another ship, the USS *Miami*, quickly steamed downriver. On April 20, Ransom's brigade captured another portion of the extensive Federal works protecting the city, and the remaining Federals retreated into their last defensive position. Hoke called for a truce and sent a courier asking for the surrender of the Federals. The 2,500 Federal soldiers laid down their arms and were escorted to prison, many to perish. Plymouth belonged to the Confederates and became the new mooring of the CSS *Albemarle*.

Prison camps, North and South, were dreadful affairs. Disease and sickness ran rampant through these camps, killing scores of men each day. Once captured, a soldier gave up his rifle, cartridge box and belt. If he was a Confederate soldier, he was also stripped of anything that belonged to the United States Army. Prisoners were then loaded on railcars and usually transported to steamers to take them north. Many North Carolinians endured prison stays at Point Lookout in Maryland, Elmira in New York, Camp Chase in Ohio and Camp Douglas in Illinois. Confederate officers were often imprisoned on Johnson's Island, near Sandusky, Ohio. An estimated 12 percent of all Confederate prisoners died while incarcerated. Most died of chronic diarrhea, dysentery and pneumonia. A few were shot by the guards, and a few managed to escape. One unfortunate part of an already dismal piece of history is the use of 600 Confederate officers as human shields by the Federal government. The Federals had received word that Federal

Salisbury Prison was just one of the prisons in the Confederacy for Union prisoners of war. *North Carolina Museum of History.*

officers were being held in Charleston, South Carolina, themselves used as human shields. In truth, the Federal officers were passing through Charleston on their way to another prison camp, and the Federals on the forts in the area routinely lobbed shells into the civilian portions of the city. The Federal government chose 600 Confederate officers, including 111 from North Carolina, to be placed in front of the Federal batteries on Morris Island. No Confederates were killed by Confederate artillery fire, but Lieutenant John Cowper of the 33rd North Carolina Troops died of pneumonia in October 1864. The Confederate officers were later transferred to Fort Pulaski, Georgia, to spend the winter. Overall, eight of the Tar Heel officers perished.

North Carolina was also the site of Federal prisons, five to be exact. While the prisons in Charlotte, Goldsboro, Raleigh and Greensboro were temporary affairs, the prison in Salisbury was one of the major prisons established by the Confederacy. The first Federal prisoners arrived in Raleigh in July 1861, but local officials had no place for them. For some months, talks between the State of North Carolina and the Confederacy went on before the state purchased an old textile mill in November 1861, guards were recruited and the first 120 prisoners arrived on December 9, 1861. By May 1862, the prison held 1,400 Federal soldiers, along with a few dissidents from North Carolina and other states. Until October 1864, the prisoners fared tolerably well, with theatrical productions, baseball games and regular paroles out of the prison. However, in 1864, the prisoner exchange system broke down, and by October, the prison, designed to hold 2,500, had a population of more than 10,000. The overcrowding and poor food, the same food eaten by the Confederate guards, led to rampant disease and death. Overall, 3,501 Federal prisoners died while incarcerated at the Salisbury prison camp.

As a reward for the successful capture of Plymouth, Hoke was promoted to major general. He next moved on Washington, but on April 26, the Federals abandoned and then plundered the town. About half of the town burned at the time the Federals were leaving. Hoke wanted to tackle New Bern next, but events in Virginia called Hoke, and most of his men, north. While there was no serious fighting involved at New Bern in April 1864, the *Albemarle* did sail again, requested by Hoke to help with the investment of the city. Seven Federal gunships waited for the Confederate ironclad. Late in the afternoon of May 5, the *Albemarle* opened the fight, and the Federals fired numerous broadsides at the ironclad vessel with little apparent effect. The USS *Sassacus* then rammed the *Albemarle*. The *Sassacus* stuck fast, pulling the *Albemarle* down and causing it to take on water. A well-placed shot by the *Albemarle* destroyed one of the engines of the Federal ship, and once the steam abated, the two vessels were free of each other. At 7:30 p.m., the *Albemarle* returned to Plymouth, its steering mechanism damaged and the smokestack so riddled by shot that the jacks found it hard to keep up steam.

April 1864 also brought another raid in the mountain counties. In early April, about forty women stormed the commissary depot in Burnsville, Yancey County. The next day, somewhere between seventy-five and two hundred men, nominally under the command of Confederate deserter Montreval Ray, stormed into town. The local Confederate enrolling officer was wounded and driven from town. Rifle stockpiles for the home guard were taken, and local merchants were abused until they revealed the location of food. About a week later, on April 15, Confederate soldiers from Asheville arrived, under the command of Colonel John B. Palmer, who had replaced Robert B. Vance as commander of the Department of Western North Carolina, and drove out the dissidents. The former home of John W. McElroy was supposedly used as a hospital for those wounded on both sides. Events like the Burnsville Raid would become all too common over the next few months.

While somewhere around 125,000 North Carolinians joined the Confederate army, there were a few who chose to join the Union army instead. Some slipped off in the early days of the war and joined the Federal army, often serving in regiments from Kentucky and Tennessee. Others

Built circa 1860 by John W. McElroy, this house, according to local history, served as a hospital after the April 1864 skirmish in Burnsville. *Author's collection.*

waited and joined local organizations. The first of the regiments of "home Yankees" was the 1st North Carolina Infantry, created in New Bern on June 7, 1862, and composed of men from the eastern counties of the state. This was the only North Carolina Federal regiment for about a year. The 1st North Carolina Colored Troops was organized in June 1863 and also was composed of men, mostly former slaves, from the eastern portions of North Carolina. The 2nd North Carolina Mounted Infantry (there was no 1st North Carolina Mounted Infantry) was organized of western Unionists in October 1863 in Knoxville, Tennessee. That same month, the 2nd North Carolina Colored Troops was also formed in Portsmouth, Virginia. The 2nd Regiment, North Carolina Infantry, was created in November 1863 in New Bern but in 1865 was consolidated with the 1st Infantry. In March 1864, the 1st North Carolina Colored Heavy Artillery was organized in New Bern and Morehead City. The 3rd North Carolina Colored Troops was organized in Norfolk, Virginia, on January 30, 1865. There were also scores of Confederate prisoners who joined organizations like the United States Volunteers, six different regiments recruited for duty out west and the United States Navy. Many former slaves from the central and western counties joined the 40th United States Colored Troops. Getting an accurate number of North Carolinians who served in Union regiments is a challenging task, considering how many joined different regiments, and a few under assumed names. It is hard to estimate how many men served in the Union army from North Carolina during the war, but between 6,000 and 7,000 would be a fair estimate.

Another raid in the western part of the state took place in June 1864. Captain George W. Kirk, a Tennessee native and member of the 2nd North Carolina Mounted Infantry who was in the process of trying to create the 3rd North Carolina Mounted Infantry, selected 130 men, mostly armed with Spencer Repeating Rifles, and set out from Morristown, Tennessee, to raid Camp Vance, near Morganton. Camp Vance was a location for collecting conscripts from western North Carolina to be forwarded to front line military units elsewhere. It was also a rendezvous point for the recently created North Carolina Junior Reserve, composed of seventeen-year-old males. There were somewhere around 250 junior reserves in camp, in the process of being organized into companies but still without arms. Kirk's movements went undetected. About daybreak on June 28, Kirk sent Camp Vance a surrender demand that was declined. A skirmish broke out, in which 12 men were killed and an untold number wounded. Soon, the camp surrendered, and Kirk nabbed 277 prisoners. His men then set about burning all the buildings, destroying 1,200 arms but saving the hospital. Soon thereafter, Kirk moved his men a short distance to the terminus of the Western North Carolina Railroad, where he found an engine and three cars, along with a stockpile of grain, all of which were burned. Instead of completing the rest of his mission, including the destruction of the bridge over the Yadkin River and the liberation of the prisoners at Salisbury, Kirk chose to return to east Tennessee. In a skirmish near the foot of Brown's Mountain, William W. Avery, one of North Carolina's leading Secessionists, was killed. Kirk is rumored to have set some of his prisoners in front of his own men to be used as human shields during the skirmish. Due to superior firepower and a well-chosen position, Kirk was able to fend off his attackers. Once back in Mitchell County, he burned the home of Colonel John B. Palmer and destroyed the Cranberry Iron Mines. The daring raid netted Kirk some 40 new recruits for his regiment and liberated 32 black men, many of whom later joined the Federal army.

During these dark days of the war, there were some remarkable Tar Heel women whose actions merit special mention. Emeline Pigott, born in Carteret County in 1836, not only served as a nurse but also participated in several clandestine operations during the war. In some instances, she employed local fishermen to gather information on the Federal fleet. In

Emeline Pigott served not only as a nurse at Morehead City but also as a spy, sending Confederate officials notice of Federal activities in the area. *North Carolina State Archives.*

1865, she was arrested and chose to eat a message while waiting for a white woman to conduct a search of her person. She was imprisoned for a short time in the jail in New Bern. Known as the Florence Nightingale of the South, Laura Wesson was just a teenager when she arrived in High Point. Wesson served as a nurse at the local wayside hospital and eventually nursed soldiers with smallpox. Wesson contracted and died of the disease herself and is buried in Oakwood Cemetery in High Point among the soldiers she so lovingly tended. Rose Greenhow, the celebrated spy who spent six months in the Old Capital Prison in Washington, D.C., was returning from Paris in October 1864 when her ship was chased by the Federals off Cape Fear. Against the wish of the captain of her vessel, Greenhow was placed on a rowboat and headed toward the North Carolina coast. Her boat was swamped, and Greenhow, possibly weighed down with money and ciphers, drowned. Her body was taken to the cottage of Mrs. Lamb, wife of the commander in charge of area defenses. The following day, she was buried in Oakdale Cemetery with full military honors. Malinda Blalock, from the Caldwell-Watauga County area, chose to enlist with her husband in the 26th North Carolina Troops in March 1862. Malinda cut off her hair, donned men's clothing and served under the name of Sam. Keith was discharged on April 20, 1862, and "Sam," not wanting to be left behind, confessed to

Rose O'Neil Greenhow was probably the most famous of the spies for the Confederacy. She drowned off the North Carolina coast in 1864. *Library of Congress.*

regimental commander Colonel Zebulon Vance. She was also discharged. The Blalocks returned to western North Carolina. They eventually became guides on a type of underground railroad that helped escaped Union prisoners and dissidents reach the Federal lines in Kentucky and Tennessee.

Many are familiar with the famous Underground Railroad that operated for decades through the eastern and central portions of North Carolina prior to the war. Places like the Great Dismal Swamp, Snow Camp in Alamance County and the New Garden community of Guilford County were all "connected" to this corridor to freedom for slaves. During the war, another underground railway sprang up. The mountains of western North Carolina became an area of passage, albeit not as safe as the Northern media had portrayed it, for men who escaped from the prisoner camps in Salisbury and Columbia, South Carolina. Some men wandered through a virtual wilderness, hoping to find friendly people to provide food and directions. Others used established routes with guides. One such route ran from Blowing Rock, over Grandfather Mountain and into Banner's Elk. In Blowing Rock, the guides were often Keith and Malinda Blalock. Once at Banner's Elk, travelers were met by other guides, like Dan Ellis, who took them farther west. In the early part of the war, the escapees were often taken to eastern Kentucky. After east Tennessee was captured by the Federals in the fall of 1863, a place like Strawberry Plains was the final destination. Other routes ran through Marion, Spruce Pine and along the Nolichucky River, and also through Hendersonville and eventually the Great Smoky Mountains. Often the escaped Federals, and at time dissidents from the central counties trying to escape, would attempt to stay with slaves, whom they found sympathetic. Seldom were slaves found on this underground railroad. Even when slaves implored the Federals to take them with them, they were refused. The slave owners might discover the slaves missing and begin to search, and the last thing an escaped Federal soldier wanted was for someone to be looking for him. Being caught with escaped slaves usually meant hanging on the spot. At times, escapees found lodging with local Unionists, who provided food and asylum, while waiting for guides. The home guard battalions were usually zealous in their attempts to find escapees and their guides. Shootouts occasionally happened, and large groups of escapees were confined to the

Keith and Malinda Blalock both served in the 26th North Carolina Troops. Keith later served in the 10th Michigan Cavalry. *Avery County Historical Museum.*

jails in Boone, Burnsville and Asheville. Major Harvey Bingham of the Watauga County Home Guard was so ardent in his search for draft dodgers and escapees that the North Carolina General Assembly voted him a letter of thanks in 1864.

Holden and the Peace Party continued to gain popularity throughout 1864. Holden declared himself a candidate for governor, running against Vance. After the votes were tallied, Vance won a second term by an even greater margin than in the election where he defeated Johnston. However, in the congressional election, only two of the ten incumbents won reelection. Of North Carolina's ten representatives, six were members of the Peace Party, including James T. Leach, one of the most outspoken leaders of the peace movement. Leach was a doctor, a prominent Johnson County slave owner and an opponent to secession. He was elected to the second Confederate Congress in late 1863. In 1864, Leach introduced a resolution into Congress reading, "That whenever the Government of the United States shall signify its willingness to recognize the reserved rights of the States and guarantee to the citizens of the States their rights of property…we will agree to treat for

James T. Leach, a North Carolina representative in the second Confederate Congress, was one of the leading peace advocates in the South. *North Carolina Museum of History*.

peace." The resolution garnered only three votes, all from North Carolina congressmen. While the effort was tabled in Richmond, the North Carolina General Assembly introduced its own peace initiatives into both houses, and both resolutions were narrowly defeated.

Further adversely affecting the state and the war effort was the loss of the *Advance*, captured off the Cape Fear River while leaving Wilmington on September 10, 1864, by the USS *Santiago de Cuba*. The *Advance* had made at least eight successful trips between the spring of 1863 and its capture in September. It was re-designated the USS *Advance* and used as a blockader.

Another major blow came in October 1864 with the loss of the *CSS Albemarle*. For quite some time, a young naval officer, Lieutenant William B. Cushing, had been making daring raids along the coast. Cushing was possibly one of the greatest naval heroes produced by the war. He had been dismissed by the Naval Academy prior to the war but had been allowed to rejoin the navy and to work his way up the ranks. In October 1862, Cushing had captured the *Adelaide* at New Topsail Inlet. A month later, Cushing captured the town of Jacksonville, destroying the salt works near New Juliet. Cushing was promoted and then transferred to Virginia waters for a short time before being transferred back to North Carolina. In February 1864, he was in command of the USS *Monticello* and led an audacious nighttime raid on Southport, intent on capturing Brigadier General Louis Hebert. The general was not at home when Cushing came calling, so Hebert's adjutant was taken instead. Cushing boldly walked through town, taking

The CSS *Albemarle*, shown here being rammed, was built in a cornfield off the Roanoke River. *From* Harper's Weekly.

his prisoner to the boats. Confederate soldiers were all running hither and thither, preparing for a large Federal assault, and paid no attention to the group in the darkness. A month later, Cushing steamed, once again under the cover of darkness, up the Cape Fear River, with plans of capturing the ironclad *Raleigh.*

There were three ironclads constructed in Wilmington during the war. The first was the CSS *North Carolina*, a 150-foot-long, iron-plated ship that carried 150 men and four cannons. But the engines of the *North Carolina* were faulty, and the ship was used as a floating battery until sea worms ate the bottom of its hull and it sank in the Cape Fear River in September 1864. Another ship was the CSS *Raleigh*, which sailed out and attacked the Federal blockading squadron on May 6, 1864, to little effect. As the *Raleigh* was returning to its wharf, it ran aground on a sandbar and stuck fast. As the tide ebbed, the *Raleigh* sank and the weight of iron and cannons caused it to split apart. Of course, when Cushing launched his raid, he did not know that the *Raleigh* had been reduced to a rusting hulk in the Cape Fear River. Cushing spent two days in the area below Wilmington gathering information before being chased by the Confederates out of the Cape Fear River.

Cushing was picked by the secretary of the navy to lead the attack against the *Albemarle.* He took two small ships and steamed up the Roanoke Rover on the evening of October 27, 1864. The *Albemarle* was berthed at Plymouth and was a real threat to the Union stranglehold on the inner-coastal area of North Carolina. Cushing's original plan was to capture the *Albemarle*, but a dog alerted the sentries, who opened fire on Cushing and his men. Cushing took his small ship, fitted with a torpedo on a boom, and charged over the obstacles. He gained just enough space to plant the torpedo and pull the wire. The explosion tore a six-foot hole in the side of the *Albemarle* and swamped Cushing's boat. Cushing gave the order to his men to save themselves and dove into the cold waters of the Roanoke. Only Cushing and one other man escaped, with two dead and eleven captured. Cushing was later promoted for his actions. Landsman Lorenzo Denning, who did not escape, was awarded the Medal of Honor for his actions.

The bold and courageous actions of Cushing and his men led to the fall of Plymouth a couple of days later, with a large loss of naval stores, twenty-two cannons and thirty-seven prisoners. Martin Howard, a landsman on the USS *Tacony*, was awarded the Medal of Honor for bravely spiking a Confederate cannon while under fire.

On August 5, 1864, Mobile Bay, the last major Confederate port on the Gulf Coast, was captured by the Federal navy. In all reality, that left the port at Wilmington as the only major harbor for blockade runners to land their cargo. The Federal War Department was soon laying plans for the capture of Wilmington. Rear Admiral David Porter was chosen to lead the naval forces, while Major General Benjamin Butler weaseled command of the infantry from one of his subordinates. Butler's plan was to explode a ship loaded with almost three hundred tons of powder near the fort and then to attack with 6,500 Federal infantry. The powder ship landed within three hundred yards of the beach and went off at 1:40 a.m. on December 24. Fort Fisher, known also as the Gibraltar of the South, sustained no damage. Later that morning, the Federal fleet opened fire on the earthen fort, the largest of its kind, with little effect. Several guns were dismounted and the barracks were burned, but few men were killed. The earth and sod structure simply absorbed the Federal shells. The Confederate artillery did manage a few well-placed hits, taking out the boilers of both the USS *Mackinac* and the USS *Osceola* and

Major General Benjamin Butler led the failed first attack on Fort Fisher in December 1864. *Library of Congress.*

setting the USS *Pontoosuc* on fire. Several of the large Parrott rifles on board the Federal vessels burst, killing several sailors. Colonel William Lamb, the immediate commander and architect of the earthen forts in the area, only allowed his gunners to fire once every half an hour, due to a scarcity of ammunition. On December 25, the Federal navy opened again on the fort, and Federal infantry began landing on the beach. They were able to capture a couple of outpost fortifications and were just yards from Fort Fisher when they were ordered to return to the beachhead and head back to their ships. Butler had taken a look at the fort, which he perceived as almost undamaged, and with bad weather beginning to set in and darkness encroaching, plus rumors of Confederate reinforcements, he chose to retreat. About 700 of his men were not able to get off the beach until rescued by the navy on December 27. The overall first attempt to take Fort Fisher by storm had ended in a complete failure. Butler sailed away before the last of his infantry left the beach, and all of the Federal ships were headed to Beaufort by the evening of December 27.

As the Federal ships sailed away, so departed the hopes of the Confederacy. And with the dawning of a new year, the war that for so long had been on the fringes, in isolated raids in the east and the west, burst forth upon the whole state.

Chapter 5

On the Homefront
1865

The Confederacy was wrecked, and nearly everyone realized it. Atlanta had fallen, and the Federals had cut a swath of destruction across Georgia. Petersburg and Richmond were besieged, with little hope in sight. Much of the old Confederacy, like the Mississippi River, Tennessee, Georgia and the coast of North Carolina, had fallen, and thousands of brave soldiers lay under the sod on seemingly countless battlefields. Almost every family, North and South, mourned the loss of a brother, husband or father. It was painfully ironic that many of the final acts in a four-year-long nightmare would be played out in a state that had been hesitant to leave the Union.

Some, like eastern North Carolina commander Braxton Bragg, himself a Tar Heel native, believed that the Federals were gone for the foreseeable future. Fort commander Colonel William Lamb and his immediate commander, Major General William Whitting, believed that the Federals would simply refit and then return to finish the job. Lamb and Whitting were correct, and the Federal fleet, reinforced by 2,000 more infantrymen but without Butler, sailed into view on January 12, 1865. Soon thereafter, the Federal infantry began disembarking and digging a position across the peninsula above Fort Fisher. The defenders inside the fort had swelled to 1,500, but no additional ammunition had arrived. Off the coast, the Federal naval vessels moved closer to the fort than they had previously, focusing their fire on individual batteries. A little after 3:00 p.m. on January 15, the naval contingent advanced toward the fort and was easily repulsed. However, the charge of the sailors and marines distracted the defenders of the fort,

General Braxton Bragg, a Tar Heel native, was placed in command in east North Carolina right before the Federals started bombarding Fort Fisher. *Library of Congress.*

and the primary attack was quickly scaling a portion of the walls. Due to the construction methods of the fort, each gun emplacement had to be scaled, and at times, Confederate counterattacks pushed back groups of the attackers. At one point, the Federals planted their colors on the fort walls, and Confederates at Battery Buchanan opened fire, killing and wounding friend and foe alike. By 5:00 p.m., half of Fort Fisher was in Federal hands. The fort's commander, William Lamb, was wounded not long after General Whiting was wounded. Repeated telegraph messages to Bragg to launch Confederates to the north against the Federal rear went largely unanswered. By 10:00 p.m., Fort Fisher, "the Confederate Goliath," had fallen. Lamb survived his wound, but Whiting died in a prisoner of war camp. The last major Confederate port was closed. During the attack, about 400 Confederates were killed and wounded, with 1,500 taken as prisoners, while 1,200 Federals were killed and wounded.

The following day, the Confederates abandoned Forts Holmes, Johnston, Campbell and Caswell, blowing up the latter, and falling back

Capture of Fort Fisher, by J.O. Davidson, completed circa 1887. *Library of Congress.*

to Fort Anderson, parallel to Hoke's position across the Camp Fear River. It took about a month for the Federals to mount another expedition. A Federal corps under Major General John Schofield was transferred from Tennessee to the Wilmington area. Schofield tried twice to flank Hoke out of his position, starting on February 11, but was unsuccessful. Schofield then transferred men to the west bank of the Cape Fear River and moved against Fort Anderson. As soon as the Federals attacked on February 17, including a naval bombardment, Bragg ordered Fort Anderson abandoned. The Confederates fell back to Town Creek, while Hoke's men likewise fell back on the opposite side of the river. On February 20, the Federals flanked the Town Creek position, and the Confederates moved back to the north side of Northeast Creek. Hoke's men were forced to abandon Wilmington, actually fighting in the street. Military stores were burned to prevent them from falling into the hands of the Federals. Federal soldiers, the same ones who had captured Fort Fisher, entered Wilmington on February 22, 1865.

Schofield had orders to proceed to Goldsboro, but the lack of cars and wagons hampered his efforts. Instead, the Federals advanced from New Bern on March 6, running into Hoke's division positioned below Kinston on Southwest Creek. The Confederates were reinforced by men from the Army

One of the destroyed guns at Fort Fisher. *Library of Congress.*

of Tennessee on March 7, and on March 8, Hoke attacked. His men were able to push in the Federal flank, capturing some one thousand soldiers, along with artillery. Hill attacked next, but part of his command, made up of junior reserves, faltered. Hill was forced to fall back to the creek. Federal reinforcements arrived and entrenched. Hoke and Hill attacked again on March 10, but neither side's flank attack was able to make much headway against the entrenched Federal position. That evening, Bragg ordered his men to withdraw across the Neuse River.

The actions of Bragg, Hoke and Hill were designed as delaying actions, trying to prevent the joining of the Federal commands of Schofield and Major General William T. Sherman and allowing the Confederates to concentrate their scattered forces. The remnants of the Army of Tennessee were coming through South Carolina. February 16, 1865, found the 58th North Carolina drawn up in the streets of Columbia, South Carolina. The city was abandoned soon thereafter and burned. Some blamed the Confederates for setting the fire, while others blamed the Federals. It was not until the last week of February that portions of the Army of Tennessee began entering the Tar

General Joseph Johnston led Confederate forces at Bentonville and surrendered the Army of Tennessee at the Bennett farm near Durham. *Library of Congress.*

Heel State, with much of that army going into camp between Waxhaw and Charlotte. On February 22, Robert E. Lee, recently appointed commander in chief of all Confederate armies, assigned Lieutenant General Joseph E. Johnston, then living with his family in Lincolnton, as commander of the Army of Tennessee.

As Joseph Johnston assumed command, and as Bragg fought at Wyse's Forks, Sherman's army entered North Carolina. By March 8, all of his forces were in the Old North State, symbolically tearing up the tracks of the Charlotte and Wilmington Railroad and burning the railroad shops at Laurinburg. March 8 found Federal cavalry encamped just north of Fayetteville, at a junction known as Monroe's Crossroads. Confederate cavalry under Wade Hampton and Joe Wheeler scouted the Federal cavalry camp of Brigadier General Judson Kilpatrick and found a road left unguarded. The Confederates massed their men and, at daybreak on March 10, crashed into the Federal camp. Kilpatrick's men scattered, and Kilpatrick himself was almost captured, fleeing from his mistress and clad only in his nightshirt and boots. When a Southerner galloped up to ask where Kilpatrick was, the quick-thinking officer pointed to another Federal cavalryman and stammered, "There he goes, on that black horse." Kilpatrick managed to find another horse and ride out of camp, where he organized fleeing Union cavalrymen and prepared for a counterattack. Confederate cavalrymen, instead of pursuing the Federals, had stopped to plunder the Federal camp. The Federals were able to recapture their artillery and, armed with Spencer Rifles, pushed the Confederates back. In the end, the skirmish, sometimes known as "Kilpatrick's Shirt-tail Skedaddle," was a Confederate victory, clearing the Fayetteville Road.

Federal bummers—soldiers operating on the fringes of the army, foraging, stealing and looting—visited several locations in the southern portions of the state. One hundred of them, under the "command" of a major, raided Wadesboro in Anson County, with orders to "clean out the town." One pastor in the town stated that "a Mr. James C. Bennett, one of the oldest and wealthiest men in Anson County, was shot at the door of his own house because he did not give up his watch and money," which another party of soldiers had already taken. Monroe was also raided, and wagons of refugees from South Carolina were happily liberated by the bummers. At times, the bummers clashed with Confederate cavalry. Near Rockingham on March 7, a portion of Wheeler's cavalry attacked a group of foragers from the 9th Pennsylvania Cavalry, killing or capturing thirty-five soldiers.

Sherman's objective was Fayetteville, with its textile mills, railroad facilities and, most important, the armory. A small squad of fewer than one hundred Federal cavalry soldiers was sent to Fayetteville to reconnoiter the town. The troopers surprised Confederate lieutenant general Wade Hampton, who gathered a handful of Confederates and charged the Federals, driving them back in confusion, believing that there were more Confederates right around the corner. The Federals were reinforced, and the Confederates retreated out of town and across the Cape Fear River, burning the bridge as they went. Sherman ordered the arsenal demolished, although some irreplaceable machinery had already been sent to Chatham and Guilford Counties. All but one of the mills, all the warehouses and the railroad property were destroyed. One local resident recorded after the war that every house and store in the town was broken into and robbed.

Johnston was concentrating his scattered forces. Those under Bragg, fighting below Kinston, were ordered to Smithfield, and likewise, Lieutenant General William J. Hardee's forces coming from Columbia, South Carolina, were ordered to Smithfield. The Confederate troops positioned in and around Charlotte were ordered to Smithfield via the railroads. Hardee's forces chose to stop and fight a portion of the Federal army, an attempt to ascertain how much of the enemy was behind them and where the entire force was headed. Hardee's force, just under 6,000 men, chose a position near Averasboro and entrenched in two main lines. The battle opened on March 15, just south of Averasboro at Gypsy Pine. The Confederate skirmishers were pushed back. On March 16, the Confederates attacked, pushing the Federals back and also rolling up their flank. Federal reinforcements arrived, and the Confederates were pushed back and out of their first line of entrenchments. But their second line, thanks to artillery, held off repeated Federal attacks. At the end of the two days of fighting, the Federals at the Battle of Averasboro had lost 100 men killed and 582 wounded, with Confederate losses around 450. Hardee had determined that only a portion of the Federal army was in front of him and that its goal was not Raleigh but rather Goldsboro. More importantly, the fighting had pushed Sherman's two columns of men more than a day's march apart. It was the opportunity that General Johnston had been looking for.

At Smithfield, Johnston christened his motley force the "Army of the South." His command was composed of the remnants of the Army of Tennessee, along with the defenders of Charleston and Wilmington. There were soldiers from Florida, Arkansas, Alabama and even Kentucky, about 22,000 men total. There were few North Carolinians. The 58th and 60th Regiments were still in Palmer's brigade. Most of the others were in Hoke's division, with the 8th, 31st, 51st and 61st Regiments in Clingman's old brigade and the 17th, 42nd and 66th Regiments in Brigadier General William Kirkland's brigade. In Johnson Hagood's brigade were parts of the 1st North Carolina Battalion of Heavy Artillery, the 36th North Carolina, Adam's Battery and portions of the 40th Regiment. Colonel John H. Nethercutt commanded a brigade of Junior Reserves, and in McLaw's division of Hardee's Corps was Colonel Washington Hardy's brigade, composed of the 50th Regiment, 7th Regiment of Senior Reserves and the 10th North Carolina Battalion. Every Confederate regiment was woefully under strength. A typical division should have contained 8,000 to 10,000 men, yet the division to which the 58th and 60th North Carolina Troops belonged had a scant 1,181 men present for duty.

The plan of attack formulated by Johnston was to use his cavalry to continue to slow the advance of the Federals. While this was being done, Hoke's division was to block the road the Federals took, below Bentonville, while Johnston's other divisions would form at right angles in the woods to Hoke's right. When the Federals formed to drive Hoke's soldiers off the road, the masked Confederates planned to attack the Federals in the flank and sweep them from the field.

Sunday, March 19, dawned a clear, bright, rain-free day. Early on, the Confederates set about digging breastworks with only a few tools at hand. The forage details of the Federal army were up early and about their assigned tasks of stealing and plundering. They soon met with Confederate cavalry that refused to give way. Federal infantry arrived. No one—from Sherman, who was not present, on down the Federal chain of command— believed that the Confederates were preparing to take a stand. Supposing that the bummers only faced Confederate cavalry, the lead division commander informed the bummer's commanding officer, "Get your d---d bummers out of the way, and I will drive the rebels out with a skirmish line!" The lead Federal infantry brigade easily enough pushed aside the Confederate cavalry but soon afterward ran into Hoke's

Major General William T. Sherman (U.S.) led his Federal army from Atlanta to Savannah, through South Carolina and finally into North Carolina. *Library of Congress.*

main line. More Federal infantry arrived, and at noon, they advanced and were easily repulsed. Falling back, the Federals entrenched. As the rest of the Confederates arrived on the field, Johnston saw his chance and, a little before 3:00 p.m., launched his assault.

With a yell, the last grand, victorious charge by a Confederate army stepped off "with great spirit and dash." The Confederates passed over a fence and then double-quick marched, slamming into the Federal position. The Federal soldiers were pushed through a wooded ravine and ran from the field, throwing away their rifles and abandoning three cannons. The entire Federal left gave way. Federal soldiers launched a counterattack, with some success, until they themselves were flanked and forced back. Soon, Hoke advanced his division—not on the flank of the Federal right, as he asked Bragg to do, but straight at the Federal enchantments. The Federal right was surrounded but fought gallantly. At 4:30 p.m., Federal reinforcements began to arrive, and the Confederates in the rear of the Federal right flank were forced to retreat. A half hour later, another Confederate charge, albeit not as organized as the first, stepped off toward the new Federal left. Federal entrenchments and artillery double- and triple-loaded with canister hurled the Confederates back at least five times. Both armies used the cover of darkness to dig in and care for the wounded and, in some instances, bury the dead. That evening, Sherman, who for the day had failed to believe that a general engagement was taking place, finally consented and ordered the other wing of his column to turn and head for Bentonville.

Johnston, sure that the other Federal wing would be on its way, dispatched Wheeler's cavalry to disrupt their passage. There was skirmishing on March 19 at Cox's Crossroads, and the next day, at Cox's Bridge, several more running skirmishes were conducted, like the one along the Goldsboro Road. By midday, portions of the Federal reinforcements began to arrive.

Overnight, Johnston had pulled his men back to their original position and entrenched in a U-shaped formation. On the afternoon of March 20, a portion of the Federal reinforcements was able to push back a segment of Hoke's division, but the Confederate line of retreat was still open. Johnston held his position to give the Confederates time to load their wounded into trains to be transported west and to invite the Federals to attack. On March 21, the Federal right was able to turn the Confederate left, coming close to cutting that line of retreat. But a Confederate counterattack pushed the Federals back. With this close call, and with more Federals arriving, Johnston chose to retreat, and by the morning of March 22, the Confederates were across Mill Creek, leaving empty trenches. Confederate losses were 2,606 men, while the Federals claimed to have lost almost 1,600, both figures that are probably too low.

Sherman chose not to pursue Johnson, heading on toward Goldsboro instead. The Confederates abandoned Goldsboro on the afternoon of March 21. Federal soldiers began arriving on March 23 for a short period of time to rest and refit. Johnston moved his forces back toward Raleigh, while many of his wounded occupied hospitals in the capital and in Greensboro.

As the battle between Sherman and Johnston came to a close, another Federal incursion was just commencing. Major General George Stoneman's orders were to destroy the railroad and military resources in both southwest Virginia and western North Carolina. Many believed that Robert E. Lee would retreat to the west and that the purpose of the raid was, as one Federal general averred, to dismantle "the country to obstruct Lee's retreat." Stoneman's command consisted of four thousand cavalrymen, with a battery of artillery. The troopers traveled lightly and were expected to live off the countryside. On March 14, 1865, the Federals set out from Knoxville, Tennessee, crossing the North Carolina line into Watauga County on March 27–28. Later that day in Boone, the lead elements ran into portions of the home guard, and a skirmish broke out. The local guardsmen believed that they were tangling with local dissidents and not veteran Union cavalrymen. On leaving Boone, Stoneman split his force. A portion moved into Caldwell County, burning the Patterson Mill, and then moved down the Yadkin River. Stoneman's other column rode down the mountain into Wilkes County. Rain swelled the river, and Stoneman's forces were separated for three days. Finally, on April

Major General George Stoneman (U.S.) organized a raid through western North Carolina in the spring of 1865. *Library of Congress.*

2, the horsemen turned north into Virginia, where several key skirmishes were fought in Wytheville and Martinsville. Nevertheless, Stoneman's men were able to rip up the tracks and burn bridges and even threatened the town of Lynchburg.

Robert E. Lee met with Grant and surrendered the Army of Northern Virginia on April 9 at Appomattox Court House, Virginia. That same day, Stoneman's column returned to North Carolina, and the different columns were reunited in Danbury in Stokes County. On April 10, the command moved through Germantown, and Stoneman again split his troopers. A portion under the command of Colonel William Palmer was to proceed to Salem, with orders to destroy the railroad bridges between Danville, Virginia, and Greensboro, along with any stockpiles of supplies they found. The second column, led by Stoneman himself, was to proceed to Salisbury.

At Salem, local residents, warned of the impending approach of the Federal soldiers, hid papers and books from the courthouse, food and other items, like cloth and animals. A small skirmish was fought on the outskirts of town, and the troopers rushed into Salem, expecting to be fired on from every building. They instead found a mostly Unionist population glad to see blue coats. Palmer then split his men up, with orders to knock out the railroad north of Greensboro and also to the south at Jamestown and at High Point. At Jamestown, not only was the railroad brigade destroyed, but so were the depot and seven cars loaded with weapons, cotton, flour and other foodstuffs. A different column arrived on the outskirts of Greensboro and charged the unpicketed camp of the 3rd South Carolina Cavalry, killing one Confederate and capturing forty-eight more. Another column captured and torched the railroad at High Point. Yet an additional column succeeded in burning the bridge over Abbott's Creek but was chased off by Confederate cavalry. By dusk on April 11, most of the detachments had returned, and Palmer moved out of Salem.

Stoneman's column proceeded south, out of Salem, ransacking Bethania and then crossing the Yadkin at Shallow Ford at 7:00 a.m. on April 11. A skirmish was fought outside Mocksville, and after taking what they needed, the Federals pushed on. They stopped that evening just twelve miles from Salisbury. After a short rest, Stoneman moved on, eventually splitting his force to invest Salisbury. Salisbury, one of the largest military depots remaining in the South, was protected by artillery, regular Confederates, government employees, home guard and even a few galvanized Yankees, former Federal prisoners who had joined the Confederate army to escape prison life—maybe 5,000 men total. The Confederates were posted behind Grant's Creek. After fierce fighting, the Confederates were flanked out of their position and fled through town, where skirmishing continued to take place. By noon on April 12, Salisbury was in Federal hands. As with other places the Federals passed through, Salisbury was pillaged. A vast supply of military stores, estimated worth $7 million, was burned, along with numerous buildings, and the offices of the *Carolina Watchman* were damaged. The infamous prison was mostly empty, the Federal prisoners having been transferred a month before. One high-priority target in the area was the 660-foot-long railroad bridge over the Yadkin River, about four miles from Salisbury. Confederate forces constructed defenses on the Davidson County side of the bridge, naming them Fort York. Only 1,200 troops manned the works. The Federals brought artillery captured at Salisbury to battle with Confederate artillery in the fort. In the end, the Confederates held, and the bridge was saved. Stoneman's troopers had to be content with destroying the rails between Salisbury and the Yadkin River bridge.

Their work in Salisbury complete, the Federals moved west to Statesville, where once again military storehouses were razed. Stoneman continued with one column west through Taylorsville and Lenoir. At Lenoir, Stoneman took his one thousand prisoners and, on April 17, continued north through Watauga County and into Tennessee. After Stoneman had left Watauga County in March, a brigade composed partially of home Yankees occupied the county, building five forts to guard the mountain passes and protect Stoneman's line of retreat. These troops terrorized citizens in the surrounding counties. The home of Jonathan Horton, Watauga County's representative in the General Assembly, was robbed an estimated eighteen times in fourteen days by Federal soldiers. Stoneman's second column proceeded to Lincolnton, skirmishing the entire time with Confederate cavalry who had refused to surrender in Virginia.

Stoneman ordered his men at Lenoir to proceed west to Asheville. The Federals skirmished successfully with local troops at Rocky Ford on the Catawba River, and soon Morganton was in Federal hands. After pillaging the town, the Federals continued west toward Asheville. On April 20, they found Swannanoa Gap obstructed and set about flanking the position, moving through Rutherfordton on April 21. On April 23, the Federal and Confederate commanders met near Asheville. The local Confederate commander, Brigadier General James Martin, had heard of the surrender of Lee and Johnston. On April 25, the Confederates agreed to a cease-fire. Many of the Federal troops and commanders departed for Tennessee thereafter. But on April 26, some of the Federal troopers returned to Asheville and sacked it.

Asheville had been attacked already once that month. On April 3, 1,100 men had moved south from Greenville, Tennessee, and into Warm Springs in Madison County. On April 6, locals put together a force of 300 men, with two cannons and manned defensive works on Woodfin Ridge, which overlooked Asheville. The battle opened at three o'clock that afternoon, and by eight o'clock that evening, the Federals were retreating back to Tennessee.

While the proposal might not have been genuine, some thought that Asheville would make a good replacement capital for the Confederate government. Richmond, Virginia, had fallen on April 3, 1865, and Jefferson Davis and the Confederate cabinet were on the run. Lee surrendered his army six days later at Appomattox. Davis, at Danville, Virginia, decided that Charlotte would be a better location, plus, Davis's wife and children were already in the Queen City, along with the remaining Confederate treasury, deposited at the old mint building. By 11:00 p.m. on April 10, Davis was on his way to Greensboro. As the train arrived in Greensboro, some of Stoneman's troopers burned the bridge behind them. Due to the large number of refugees, wounded and paroled soldiers and fears of Union reprisals, Davis had great difficulty finding a single room to occupy. Other members of the cabinet were forced to stay on the train, spending much of their time in a leaky boxcar dubbed the "Cabinet Car." Davis denied that the reports he received were as grim as the writers told. The president called General Johnston to Greensboro for a consultation. Davis wanted to raise a new army to continue the fight; Johnston wanted permission to open negations with Sherman. Most of the cabinet, with Davis and Johnston, met on April 12. Once again, Davis wanted to continue, while everyone else sided with Johnston, save one. Davis gave his consent but chose to continue south and west, attempting to link up with Confederates beyond the Mississippi River. Davis and his cabinet left Greensboro on horseback and wagons on April 15, arriving in Lexington the next day. They were in Salisbury on the seventeenth, Concord on the eighteenth and finally Charlotte. While standing in front of the home of Lewis Bates and making an impromptu speech, Davis learned of the assassination of Abraham Lincoln, a communiqué that visibly shook him. The Confederate government set up at the Bank of North Carolina, and on April 26, Davis held the last full meeting of the Confederate cabinet at the home of W.F. Phifer. After the meeting, Davis set out with a large contingent of Confederate cavalry heading south, toward Texas, but was captured on May 10 near Irwinsville, Georgia, by members of Stoneman's command.

Most of the official Confederate records that had not already been destroyed in the conflagration that consumed Richmond were abandoned in Charlotte or the surrounding countryside. Some were destroyed, while others disappeared. The records of the State and War Departments were left under the care of Samuel Cooper, Confederate adjutant and inspector general, who chose not to proceed south with Davis. At the end of the war, at least eighty crates of records were turned over to Federal authorities.

Joseph Johnston used the lull after the battle of Bentonville to reorganize his army. Many regiments, only the size of a company or two, were consolidated. Johnston renamed his command the Army of Tennessee. On April 7, Johnston reported that he had 30,424 men present. Johnston's command passed through Raleigh on April 11 and skirmished with the Federals near Raleigh and at Morrisville on April 13. Sherman's Federal troops entered Raleigh later that day, firing off signal rockets from the top of the state capitol. On April 14, Johnston opened communications with Sherman while still moving his army west and skirmishing with the Federals at Sander's Farm. The armies skirmished again in Chapel Hill on April 15. By April 16, the Confederates were passing through Greensboro, mingling with the parolees from the Army of Northern Virginia. While in Greensboro, many of Confederates were issued new clothing to prevent the material from destruction like that in Salisbury. On April 17, Sherman and Johnston met outside Durham at the farm owned by the Bennett family. It was there that Johnston learned of the death of Lincoln. When Sherman's men learned of the tragic event, many wanted to torch Raleigh and continue pursuing the Confederates, willing to "reenlist for 40 years to exterminate the Southern race." Federal solders were not allowed to leave camp, and Sherman gave orders to his provost to shoot any who did.

The first set of terms reached by Sherman and Johnston was rejected by President Andrew Johnson and his cabinet on April 21. Sherman was trying to get Johnston to surrender all the remaining Confederate armies in the field, along with civil authorities. Sherman had overstepped his boundaries, and General Grant was sent to Raleigh to confer with, or guide, Sherman.

The truce between Johnston and Sherman was set to expire when Johnston called for another meeting with Sherman at the Bennett farm. On April 26, Sherman presented the same terms that Grant had offered to Lee at Appomattox, terms that Johnston accepted. The Army of Tennessee surrendered and, on May 1, the men began to receive their paroles and

Sherman and Johnston met at the Bennett farm outside Durham where Johnston surrendered the Army of Tennessee. *From* Harper's Weekly.

head home. As a final act, General Johnston paid his men with some of the Confederate treasury that was left in his protection as Davis and his party moved through the state. Each former Confederate soldier under Johnston's command received $1.17 in Mexican silver, along with cloth, thread and yarn, to take home or to trade for food along the way.

Word of the end of hostilities was slow to reach some areas of the state. After the fall of Asheville, Confederate departmental commander James G. Martin moved his headquarters to Waynesville in Haywood County. By May 3, elements of Thomas's Legion had joined up at Balsam Gap. Martin left five companies at Balsam Gap and moved the other five to Soco Gap. On May 6, Martin learned that there were Federals in Waynesville. William Thomas was dispatched with six companies to the town. After reaching the town and concealing themselves, Thomas sent a scout out to look over the town. He also decided to call for the other companies of his command and dispatched fifty men under the command of Lieutenant Robert Conley to move via White Sulphur Springs and make contact. Deep in the woods, Conley ran into a group of Federal soldiers at the springs just west of Waynesville. Conley's men formed and fired into the Federals, killing James Arrowood and routing the Federals. That evening, Thomas's men took control of two of the most prominent peaks in the area. The next day, the Federal commander in Waynesville asked to meet with Martin. The Confederates agreed, and Martin, Thomas and twenty Cherokees, complete with war paint and tomahawks, arrived. Thomas wanted to ride swiftly into Waynesville, unleashing the Cherokees to scalp the Federals. The Federal commander advised Martin that such actions would lead to retribution. The Confederates finally agreed to surrender, and on May 9, the Cherokees signed their paroles and drifted back into the mountains.

Former Confederate soldiers were returning to their homes along the coves and hamlets in the east and the hollows and mountainsides in the west. Some had been gone for four years, and many were unrecognizable to their families as they shuffled along. A little five-year-old girl recalled seeing "a part of a defeated army, a long line of men, poorly clad, march[ing] up the streets in Lincolnton from the old depot. Some were halt and lame, and some with one arm or one eye…They had braved many battles and left many comrades slain on bloody fields. They came home discouraged by defeat and found the country impoverished." She took "all the roses in the garden and as these brave men in defeat walked by I handed out roses to them."

Chapter 6

Tar Heels to the Front

First at Bethel, furthest at Gettysburg and Chickamauga and last at Appomattox" is a phrase that is often used to encapsulate the role of North Carolinian's Confederate soldiers. But the part played by Tar Heels in the battles of the Civil War goes far beyond Bethel, Gettysburg, Chickamauga and Appomattox.

On May 11, 1861, ten volunteer companies encamped at the fairgrounds in Raleigh were organized into the 1st North Carolina Volunteers, with Colonel Daniel H. Hill commanding. By the end of the month, North Carolina's first Confederate regiment was stationed in Richmond, Virginia. The 1st Volunteers soon found themselves on the Peninsula to the southeast of Richmond, serving as a barrier between the Confederate capital and the still Federally controlled tip of the isthmus. In June 1861, the Federals sought to expand their foothold and launch an expedition up the Peninsula. The 4,400-man Federal force encountered the 1st Volunteers, several pieces of artillery and portions of the 3rd Virginia Infantry, about 1,400 men total, in the earthworks near Bethel Church. The Federal attacks were ill coordinated and, at the end of the day, beaten back. Federal loses were 18 killed and 53 wounded, while the Confederates lost 1 killed and 10 wounded. The lone Confederate fatality was Henry Wyatt, struck in the head while trying to flush Federals out of a building. The Federal forces retreated back to their base at Fortress Monroe, while the Confederates also redeployed into the works around Yorktown. Henry Wyatt was taken to Richmond, given a hero's funeral and interred in Hollywood Cemetery, lamented as the first battlefield death of the Confederacy.

Private Henry Wyatt, 1st North Carolina Volunteers, was killed at the Battle of Big Bethel, Virginia, in June 1861. *North Carolina State Archives.*

Bethel was barely old news when the forces in blue and gray met again, this time on the plains of Manassas not far from Washington, D.C. The 6th North Carolina Troops had remained in North Carolina long enough to serve as an escort for the body of Governor Ellis before arriving in the Shenandoah Valley. They were assigned to the brigade of Brigadier General Barnard Bee. On July 18, the brigade was ordered to Manassas to reinforce the Confederate forces. A Federal force of thirty-three thousand men was advancing south from Washington, D.C., and the Confederates along Bull Run needed reinforcements. The Tar Heels arrived on July 21 and soon found themselves charging up Henry House Hill toward a Federal battery. Colonel Charles Fisher, their commander, was killed while "gallantly leading his men." The 6th North Carolina was forced back but charged again, only to fall back once more, leaving the Federal battery between the lines. Late that afternoon, the 6th North Carolina was called upon to help pursue the retreating Federals. At the end of the day, the 6th North Carolina lost twenty-three killed and fifty wounded.

While the two principal armies in Virginia took time to reorganize, military actions flared up in other theaters of the war. Southern forces won victories at Wilson's Creek, Missouri, in August and Ball's Bluff, Virginia, in October. Federal forces were victorious at Rich Mountain in western Virginia in July,

This silk banner, belonging to the 5th North Carolina State Troops, was the first Confederate battle flag captured during the war. It was taken on May 5, 1862, during the Battle of Williamsburg, Virginia. *North Carolina Museum of History*.

Cheat Mountain in western Virginia in September and Port Royal Sound in South Carolina in November. For North Carolinians, the war came home with the loss of the forts at Hatteras Inlet on the Outer Banks in August. The new year dawned bleakly for Confederate forces, with losses at Mill Springs, Kentucky, in January; Roanoke Island and New Bern in eastern North Carolina in February and March; and Forts Henry and Donelson along the Tennessee River in February. A major battle at Shiloh, Tennessee, in April resulted in yet another Confederate loss. Also lost were Confederate fortifications along the middle Mississippi River and at Pea Ridge, Arkansas, in March 1862. Fort Pulaski, guarding the mouth of the Savannah River, fell in April, as did New Orleans. None of these reversals involved rank-and-file Tar Heel soldiers.

Spring 1862 brought a major Federal incursion into Virginia. A substantial force landed at Fortress Monroe and forced the Confederate defenders out of the Yorktown defenses. Portions of the Confederate army fought a delaying action at Williamsburg. The 5th North Carolina Troops, along with the other regiments of Jubal Early's brigade, made a desperate charge upon the pursuing Federals, causing Daniel Hill to remark, "The slaughter of the 5th N.C. regiment was one of the most awful things I ever saw." Losses were 302 dead, wounded and captured. Their sacrifice compelled the Federals to slow their advance, but they were soon poised just east of Richmond, almost

100,000 strong. Another Federal force of 40,000 was stationed to the north of Richmond at Fredericksburg.

By mid-May 1862, the primary Confederate army in Virginia contained just eighteen Tar Heel regiments scattered throughout the army, save for five regiments in Lawrence Branch's brigade, recently transferred from the Kinston area. Branch's Brigade was stationed near Hanover, guarding railroads. On May 27, a Federal corps with orders to eliminate the Confederates between the two Federal commands located to the south and north attacked Branch's forces. Three of Branch's units, the 18th, 28th and 37th Regiments, suffered heavily, and Branch was forced to retreat back toward Richmond. A couple of days later, Confederate commander Joseph Johnston pitched into the Federals at Seven Pines, also called Fair Oaks, attempting to destroy an isolated portion of the Federal army. At the forefront of the battle was the 4th North Carolina State Troops, which lost 369 men killed, wounded and missing, while the colonel of the 16th Regiment, Champion Davis, was killed. During the battle, Johnston was wounded and replaced by Robert E. Lee. Over the next three weeks, Lee sought to strengthen his command, and

Ensign Emanuel Rudisill, color-bearer of the 16th North Carolina State Troops, with his flag. *Library of Congress.*

thousands of troops, including thirty-eight Tar Heel regiments, joined the newly christened Army of Northern Virginia.

Lee launched a series of attacks at the end of June that drove the Federal army back down the Peninsula. North Carolinians were found at the forefront of many of these engagements, with staggering losses. On June 26, at Mechanicsville, Lee attacked a portion of the Federal army separated by the Chickahominy River. Lee was unable to get more than one-third of his army into the battle. Even though the attack was a Confederate failure, the Federal army began to retreat to a new position near Gaines Mill. Lee again attacked but failed to get his division commanders to work together. Toward the end of the day, the Federal lines were broken. The 20th North Carolina Troops of Garland's Brigade, Daniel Hill's division, lost 272 men while charging the entrenched Federal position. Once again, the Federal army took up a new line of defense, just a little farther away from Richmond. Smaller battles at Garnett's Farm and Savage Station followed. On June 30, portions of Lee's army fought at Glendale or Frayser's Farm. The attacks were initially successful, but the Federals counterattacked, and

Jesse S. Barnes hailed from Wilson County and served as captain in Company F, 4th North Carolina State Troops. Barnes was killed at Seven Pines on May 21, 1862. *Library of Congress.*

the Confederates were forced to retreat. Colonel Charles Lee of the 37th North Carolina was killed during the attack. Finally, the Federals retreated to a position known as Malvern Hill. On July 1, Lee attacked the entrenched position and, after repeated assaults, failed to carry the position. However, the Federals no longer posed a threat to the Confederate capital and soon retreated even farther down the Peninsula.

New threats soon emerged north of Richmond, and Tar Heel soldiers found themselves engaged at Cedar Mountain on August 9. It was here that Branch's North Carolina brigade helped save the vaunted Stonewall Brigade, turning the battle into a Confederate victory. Lee continued to transfer his army north to drive the Federals out of central Virginia before they could link up with the Federals transferring off the Peninsula and into the Washington, D.C. area. Two weeks later, Stonewall Jackson marched around the flank of the Federal army and captured the Federal supply depots at Manassas Gap. On August 29, the Federals attacked Jackson's men on the old Manassas battlefield, and on August 30, the Federals suffered a

Members of the 2nd North Carolina State Troops killed in the fighting in the Sunken Road at Sharpsburg, near Antietam Creek. *Library of Congress.*

humiliating defeat. At the time of the Battle of Second Manassas, Lee's army only fielded fifteen North Carolina regiments, but once again, the Tar Heels were in the forefront of the battle. After fighting a small engagement on the outskirts of Washington at Chantilly, Lee turned his army north, crossing the Potomac River on September 4. A sharp fight ensued on September 14 at South Mountain, as the Federals, who had gained a copy of Lee's plan of battle, cut through the mountain passes. The 15th North Carolina Troops lost 183 of 402 men engaged. The next day, Harpers Ferry, with the help of Tar Heel regiments, fell to the Confederate forces. Almost 13,000 Federal soldiers surrendered.

Since the Federals were pressing his army, Lee sought to concentrate his men at the village of Sharpsburg, near Antietam Creek. The Federals attacked Lee's left first but were never able to completely overpower the Confederates. Next they tried the center, with elements of Daniel Hill's division positioned in a sunken farm road. Part of the position was occupied by George Anderson's brigade, made up of the 2nd, 4th, 14th and 30th North Carolina Regiments. These regiments were eventually pushed out of their position, now known as the Bloody Lane, but not before stalling several Federal attacks. Anderson's brigade lost 327 killed and wounded. Late in the day, the Federals were closing in on Lee's right flank when portions of A.P. Hill's division arrived and stopped the Federal advance. Near sunset, General Branch was killed, and command of his brigade passed on to James Lane. With almost 23,000 men killed and wounded in one day, Antietam became known as the bloodiest day in American history. Both sides were numb from the losses, and little action transpired on September 18. The following day, Lee withdrew, seeking to redeploy on the Federal flanks. A rear guard action followed on September 20 near Shepherdstown. Portions of the Federal army had crossed over the Potomac River and were attempting to crush a portion of Lee's army. A charge by A.P. Hill's division drove the Federals back across the river.

For several weeks, Lee rested his army in the vicinity of Winchester, Virginia. In December, the Federal army began to move south, trying to get between Lee's army and Richmond. The lack of pontoon boats at Fredericksburg stalled the Federal army, giving Lee time to move his army to the heights overlooking the town. The Confederate left was an easily defended hill that repeatedly and easily stopped Federal charges. On the Confederate right, a six-hundred-yard swamp interrupted the Confederate line. The Federals pushed into this swamp and flanked James Lane's North Carolina brigade. After running out of ammunition, the brigade was pushed

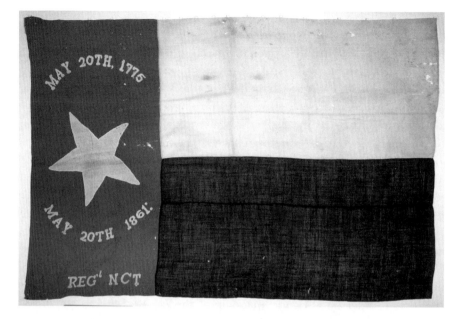

The first ten North Carolina regiments received silk state flags, while other regiments received cotton bunting flags, like this one belonging to the 30th Regiment. *North Carolina Museum of History.*

back, but reinforcements bolstered the Confederate line. The 57th North Carolina, a part of Laws's brigade of Hood's division, charged down the railroad, delivering a punishing fire at the Federals. The regiment suffered heavily, losing fifty-five killed and eighty-nine wounded. The December 13 battle of Fredericksburg was one of the worst defeats for the Union army during the war.

Most of North Carolina's Confederate regiments served in the east with the Army of Northern Virginia. Only a few served in the western theater of the war: the 29th, 39th, 58th and 60th Regiments. In November 1862, the principal Confederate army in the west, the Army of Tennessee, was positioned at Murfreesboro, just thirty miles southeast of Nashville, Tennessee. The day after Christmas, the Federals advanced, arriving in front of the Confederate lines on December 30. Both Federal and Confederate commanders adopted the same battle plan: to attack the other's right flank. The Confederates were able to attack first early on the morning of December 31 and drove portions of the Federal army back. The 29th North Carolina was in the thick of the fight. After the war, then-colonel Robert B. Vance claimed that the first loss of the day came from the 29th Regiment. The Federals were reinforced and able to establish a new line. Neither army did much on January 1. The next

Before the 39th North Carolina Troops left for Tennessee, the ladies of Asheville presented this now-battle-scarred flag to the soldiers. *North Carolina Museum of History.*

day, about 4:00 p.m., Confederate commander Braxton Bragg launched a new attack, which was repulsed. The 60th North Carolina, which was involved in the last attack of the evening of December 31, charged toward the massed Federal batteries to no avail. The 29th North Carolina lost about 60 men killed and wounded, while the 60th Regiment lost 110 men. Bragg stayed on the field until night fell on January 3, when he fell back and took up winter quarters at Shelbyville and Tullahoma, Tennessee.

Both the armies in the eastern and the western theater went into winter quarters and were inactive until the spring of 1863. In early May, the Federals in Virginia forded the Rappahannock River and began flanking the Confederates near Fredericksburg. Stonewall Jackson quickly designed a daring battle plan: to take his own corps around the Federal army and attack their right flank near Chancellorsville. While the plan left Lee with few troops to hold the Federals in his front and rear, Lee agreed, and Jackson began his renowned march. Jackson's command contained ninety infantry regiments, twenty-five of which were from North Carolina, the largest in either Confederate corps. Jackson's corps snaked around the Federal flank, while the Federal commander believed that they were in the process of retreating. At 5:00 p.m. on May 2, Jackson launched his attack, destroying the right flank of the Federal army. Darkness soon settled upon the field, and

Jackson was forced to stop and reorganize his troops. Lane's Tar Heel brigade, of A.P Hill's division, which had been in the rear, advanced and took up a position ahead of the other soldiers. Unbeknownst to Lane's men, Jackson and his staff had ridden out to reconnoiter the Federal position for a night attack. The Federals began firing at the 37th North Carolina, who returned the fire, catching Jackson between the lines. He and his party rode quickly to the north side of the Orange Plank Road and into the guns of the 18th North Carolina. Jackson was grievously wounded when struck by the smoothbore rounds from the regiment's muskets. Jackson was taken off the field and transported to a farmhouse in the Guiney's Station community, where he died on May 10. Jackson's command was turned over to cavalry commander General J.E.B. Stuart. On the morning of May 3, Stuart and Lee launched repeated assaults on the entrenched Federal lines. These constant attacks eventually pushed the Federals back; they re-crossed the river on the night of May 5–6. Estimated casualties totaled 30,051 men. According to Fox's *Regimental Losses*, seven of the top ten losses in Confederate organizations were sustained by Tar Heel regiments.

Not long after the battle, Lee began a second invasion of the North. In early June, he began moving his army north. On June 8, Lee reviewed his cavalry and then left his famed cavalry commander, J.E.B. Stuart, with orders to push across the Rappahannock River the next day and shield the Army of Northern Virginia's journey north. Before Stuart could get his men moving on June 9, the Federal cavalry launched its own attack, attempting to break up a perceived Confederate raid. The largest cavalry battle fought in North America raged for hours as each side attacked and counterattacked at Brandy Station. Stuart was forced to rush men from one portion of the field to another. There were several Tar Heel cavalry regiments involved, including the 1st North Carolina Cavalry, which was "in the thickest of the fight and the longest in the field." The regiment lost five killed, twelve wounded and fourteen missing. On the other side of the battlefield, Colonel Solomon Williams of the 2nd North Carolina Cavalry was killed during a charge late in the day. The Federals retreated across the river, and the Confederate cavalry soon began the journey north.

Lee's army continued north into Maryland and Pennsylvania. He hoped to draw the Federals out of Virginia, to supply his army from Northern farms and undermine the Lincoln administration by fueling the Northern peace movement with another Confederate victory. With Jackson's death, Lee reorganized his army. James Longstreet still commanded the First Corps. Richard Ewell took command of Jackson's corps, and A.P. Hill commanded the new Third Corps. Most of the North Carolinians were in Ewell's and Hill's commands. The Confederates captured numerous towns and were threatening Harrisburg, Pennsylvania, when Lee learned that the Federals were just a couple of days' march away. Lee ordered his scattered corps to concentrate near Cashtown, drawing the Federals away from his lines of communication. Federal cavalry was reported in Gettysburg, and two divisions of Hill's corps were sent to drive out the cavalry. Contact was made at 7:30 a.m. on July 1. Henry Heth, of Hill's corps, drove forward two brigades with little effect. Federal infantry soon arrived to strengthen them just to the west of Gettysburg. Robert Rodes of Ewell's corps arrived from the north and sent forward two of his Tar Heel brigades, under Junius Daniel and Alfred Iverson. This attack also failed, and the 20th North Carolina of Iverson's brigade suffered severely. Heth advanced three other brigades, including James Pettigrew's Tar Heel brigade. Pettigrew's 11th and 26th Regiments pitched forward, attacking the Federals on McPherson's Ridge. The 11th Regiment, coming in on the Federal flank, was mauled badly, losing more than 40 killed, including Major Egbert Ross, and 160 wounded, including Colonel Collett Leventhorpe. On the left of Leventhorpe's regiment, the 26th Regiment attacked up the ridge, meeting with even worse losses. In the

Private W.T. Harrison of Burke County served in the 11th North Carolina State Troops. *Library of Congress.*

thirty minutes it took to push off the Federals, the 26th North Carolina lost 623 of 839 men engaged, including Henry Burgwyn, their youthful colonel. Fourteen men who had picked up the colors of the regiment had been shot. William Pender's division of Hill's command arrived and pushed the Federals back, while other elements of Ewell's corps pushed from the north, giving the Confederates control of the town.

Fighting on July 2 was concentrated on the flanks of the Federal line on Cemetery Ridge. On the Confederate left, the fighting fell to John Hood's division of Longstreet's corps, which contained few North Carolinians, namely Reilly's Battery. At times, the battery was on the far right of the Confederate line. On the Confederate left, Colonel Isaac Avery's Tar Heel brigade played an important part in the dusk attack. The 6th and 57th North Carolina Regiments succeeded in pushing the Federals back, but their call for reinforcements went unheeded, and they were forced off the field. Colonel Avery was mortally wounded during the attack, penning the note "Major: Tell my father I died with my face to the enemy," as he lay alone in the smoke and darkness. Although the repeated flank attacks had failed, Lee chose to attack again on July 3. He reasoned that since the Federals had reinforced their flanks, their center must be weak. Lee cobbled together fifteen thousand men from Longstreet's and Hill's commands and, after an hour-long artillery assault, sent them toward the Federal lines on Cemetery Hill. The Federal center was not weak, and the Confederates met with great loss. Fifteen of the forty-two regiments involved were from North Carolina. While there was great debate about who went the farthest during the assault, the honor probably falls upon the 55th North Carolina. The flags of the 26th and 47th North Carolina Troops, just two of the more than sixty captured, were taken at the wall occupied by the Federals. The Battle of Gettysburg was costly to the Confederates. An estimated one-fourth of the 20,451 Confederate casualties were from North Carolina. Tar Heel native Major General William D. Pender was mortally wounded on July 2.

On July 4, the Confederates began their retreat back to Virginia. Recent rains had swollen the Potomac River, trapping Lee's army. The Confederates dug in and started to work on pontoon boats. Most of the Confederates had crossed by July 14, when the Federals launched an attack at Falling Waters. Henry Heth's division was able to repel the attack, but Brigadier General James Pettigrew was mortally wounded. Pettigrew was one of North Carolina's most promising citizens. Coupled with the loss of Vicksburg, Mississippi, on the Fourth of July, 1863 had been a devastating month for Southerners.

While the state they came from is unknown for certain, these three Confederates, likely from North Carolina, were captured following the Battle of Gettysburg. *Library of Congress*.

Brigadier General James J. Pettigrew led a division on the third day of Gettysburg and was mortally wounded at Falling Waters, Maryland, dying on July 17, 1863. *North Carolina Museum of History*.

Much of Lee's army settled down and, save for the small Mine Run campaign in November, was inactive until the spring of 1864. While Virginia was relatively quiet, the western theater was ablaze. In early September, Knoxville and most of eastern Tennessee were abandoned, except for Cumberland Gap. Brigadier General Charles Frazier was left in command of a small number of regiments, including the 62nd and 64th North Carolina Troops. On September 2, Knoxville was captured, and six days later, Cumberland Gap was surrounded. Frazier's 1,700 men surrendered on September 9, and 873 members of the 62nd and 64th Regiments were sent to Camp Douglas prison in Chicago, Illinois. Many perished during their stay in prison.

The regiments and brigades from east Tennessee were sent to reinforce Braxton Bragg and the Army of Tennessee near Chickamauga, Georgia. Unlike the Army of Northern Virginia, there were only a few Tar Heel regiments scattered throughout Bragg's army. The 29th North Carolina was in Matthew Ector's brigade; the 39th North Carolina was in Evander McNair's brigade; the 58th North Carolina was in John Kelly's brigade; and the 60th North Carolina was in Marcellus Stovall's brigade. Added to this was the 6th North Carolina Cavalry in H.B. Davidson's brigade. The 6th Cavalry spent the first couple of weeks of September skirmishing with Federal troops in north Georgia, including actions at Leet's Tan Yard and Reed's Bridge. A member of Nathan Bedford Forrest's command, the 6th Cavalry helped open the Battle of Chickamauga on September 18 and was heavily engaged on the following morning. During the morning action of September 19, Forrest sought reinforcements and, bypassing the chain of command, called upon Ector's brigade, including the 29th North Carolina. Instead of trying to sweep over the Federal lines, Ector halted his brigade and began firing volleys. After half an hour, Ector was forced to withdraw and spent the rest of the day in reserve. The 39th North Carolina, of McNair's brigade, was heavily involved on both days of the battle. By midday on September 19, McNair was supporting Bragg's endeavor to turn the Federal flank, while Bragg was fending off an attempt on his own flank, with the battle raging over the La Fayette Road for several hours. During part of the action, the 39th North Carolina, along with an Arkansas regiment, was sent to bolster the Confederate right. For a short time, the way to the Federal rear was open. The Federals, using Spencer rifles, soon saw the danger and opened a flanking fire on the Confederates, driving them back. There were other attacks throughout the late afternoon and early evening, but at the end of the day, the Confederates had pushed the

Sergeant Major Drury D. Coffey came from Caldwell County and served in the 58th North Carolina Troops. He spent the last year of the war as a prisoner. *Caldwell Heritage Museum.*

Federal army back. Overnight, the Federals sought to consolidate their lines, while Confederate reinforcements from Virginia arrived.

Bragg's plan for September 20 was for the right of the Confederate line to attack at "day-dawn," while the divisions to the left engaged once their neighbors made contact. Breckinridge's division launched the first attack and quickly landed in the rear of the Federal lines. The 60th North Carolina was in the center of the attack that pushed the Federals back. A call for reinforcements went out to follow up the successful attack, a call that went unheeded. Federal reinforcements soon arrived, and the Confederates, so close to cutting off the Federal line of retreat, were pushed back. Of the 150 men taken into the attack by the 60th Regiment, 8 were killed, 36 were wounded and 16 were reported missing. As the attack rolled down the Confederate line, the 29th North Carolina and Ector's brigade were engaged in supporting roles. On the Confederate left, James Longstreet had massed 10,000 Confederate soldiers. The Federals had shifted men to bolster their left, making a sizeable hole in their line, when Longstreet launched his attack. The 39th North Carolina was in the front, on the right. According to the Official Records, the 39th Regiment "drove the enemy steadily and rapidly back, passing over two successive lines of temporary breastworks, a distance of about three-quarters of a mile." Soon, the regiment came upon two batteries and captured ten pieces of artillery, losing 100 killed and wounded. Colonel Coleman replaced the wounded McNair as brigade commander. The Federal right collapsed; a secondary position was taken on Horseshoe Ridge, and the Confederates made several attempts to dislodge the Federals from this spot. Late in the day, Bragg called upon his last reserve, Preston's division, including the 58th North Carolina. The 58th Regiment charged, coming out of the woods at an angle to the Federal line. The right side of the regiment was quickly chewed up. Edmond Kirby, promoted to lieutenant colonel the day before, was killed. Regimental commander John Palmer rallied his men and eventually moved to the far left for another charge. While the 58th Regiment was charging, the men met in the falling darkness a Federal regiment coming down the hill. Both sides broke off the attack, and the Federals retreated back to Chattanooga throughout the night. The 58th Regiment spent the night on Snodgrass Hill, having lost 161 killed, wounded and missing.

Following the battle, Bragg reorganized his army. The 58th and 60th Regiments were assigned to Brigadier General Alexander Reynolds's brigade, and the 29th and 39th Regiments were transferred to the Department of Mississippi and East Louisiana. The 6th North Carolina Cavalry was sent to east Tennessee. Bragg was able to bottle the Federals up at Chattanooga, besieging the city. By the end of October, the Federals had managed to break the siege and obtain supplies. The Confederates were unable to close the line. In late November, the Federals attacked at Tunnel Hill and Lookout Mountain and at Missionary Ridge on November 25. The 58th and 60th Regiments were at the base of Missionary Ridge, with orders to fire a volley and then retreat. Unfortunately, not all Confederate brigades received the same orders. Reynolds's brigade managed to trade volleys for an hour, with the Federals falling back and regrouping. Reynolds then ordered his men to retreat. Other regiments held on until being overpowered. Once on top of Missionary Ridge, Reynolds's brigade was disorganized, some men finding a place on the front line and others in a reserve position near Bragg's headquarters. The Federals eventually made their way up the mountain, and the Confederate line collapsed. No official losses were reported for either regiment. Reynolds's brigade went into winter camp near Dalton, Georgia. Their winter repose was briefly interrupted in February 1864 when they were involved in the first Battle of Dalton, with minor losses for both regiments.

Sergeant Major Parker D. Robbins, a literate, property-owning free person of color from Bertie County, served in the 2nd United States Colored Cavalry. He also served in the 1868 constitutional convention. *North Carolina State Archives.*

With the two principal Confederate armies inactive until May, the war moved elsewhere. In early 1863, there was a movement to raise regiments of African Americans to fight for the Union. Federal troops stationed in eastern North Carolina believed that an entire such brigade could be raised there. Work began in the spring of 1863 on organizing the 1st North Carolina Colored Volunteers (NCCV), made up largely of escaped slaves and refugees from coastal towns and counties. The regiment was soon in South Carolina and, in February 1864, transferred to Jacksonville, Florida. The Federal expedition commander set off west, hoping to cut the railroad over the Suwannee River and stop the flow of Confederate supplies north. The 1st NCCV was brigaded with the 54th Massachusetts Infantry under the command of Colonel James Montgomery. Once the Confederates were found drawn up in a line of battle just west of the village of Olustee, the Federal plan was to hold their attention to the front with two regiments and artillery while a brigade was sent to roll up the flank. Montgomery's brigade was held in reserve. However, a Federal regiment sent to the front crumpled under the Confederate attack, and the Federal commander sent in the remaining regiments in a piecemeal fashion. In a final act, Montgomery's brigade was called into action, double-quicking the last six or seven miles to the battlefield. The 1st NCCV went into action on the left, with the 54th Massachusetts on the right. Portions of the 7th Connecticut Infantry were in the center. The actions of these men saved the Federal army from a complete rout, and the Federals were able to retreat back to Jacksonville. The 1st NCCV lost 230 men during the battle, along with regimental commander Lieutenant Colonel William N. Reed. The 1st NCCV, re-designated the 35th United State Colored Troops in February, spent most of the year in Florida, battling small numbers of Confederates and mosquitoes and performing garrison duty. They were transferred back to South Carolina in November 1864.

Spring always brought action with the large armies, and 1864 was no different. Two different Federal offensives were launched in May 1864: one in Virginia and the other in Georgia. In Virginia, the Federal army moved across the Rapidan River, hoping to clear some woods and outflank the Army of Northern Virginia. The Confederates moved swiftly, and the Federals were caught in the Wilderness, unable to bring their superior numbers to bear. The fighting started early on the morning of May 5 as the 47th North Carolina Troops skirmished with the 5th New York Cavalry, pushing them back along the Orange Plank Road. Soon, all of William Kirkland's North Carolina brigade was involved. Most of the Battle of the Wilderness was confined to seesaw fighting in the tangled woods and a few clearings in the area. During one of those struggles, the 45th North Carolina, of Junius Daniel's brigade, captured Federal artillery in Saunder's Field. Those guns were later "captured" again by the 1st North Carolina State Troops. After repelling numerous attacks throughout the day, Kirkland ordered his brigade to charge but was unable to penetrate the Federal lines and was forced to fall back. The 46th North Carolina, attacking to the south of the Orange Plank Road, along Poplar Run, reportedly lost 39 killed and 251 wounded out of 540 men engaged. Colonel William Saunders and Major Neill McNeill were wounded. Day two started with an attack on the Confederate right, and A.P. Hill's corps was pushed back by the Federals. Colonel Clark Avery of the 33rd Regiment was mortally wounded, and the colors of the 13th Regiment were captured by the 141st Pennsylvania Infantry. Longstreet's corps soon arrived, and while Longstreet was wounded by friendly fire, his men were able to stabilize the Confederate right and even push the Federals back. On the Confederate left, an attack launched late in the day also pushed the Federals back. A part of the attacking force was the North Carolina brigade

This Second National Confederate flag was used by the 13th North Carolina Troops until its capture in May 1864 at the Battle of the Wilderness. *North Carolina Museum of History.*

of Robert Johnston, composed of the 5th, 12th, 20th and 23rd Regiments. On May 5, the brigade had been at Taylorsville, above Richmond, and according to Captain V.E. Turner of the 23rd Regiment, "by the quickest forced march on record covered sixty-six miles in twenty-three hours." Johnston's brigade attacked near dusk and pushed back the Federal right flank. At the end of two days of fighting, the battle had become a stalemate. The Federals had wanted to push through the Wilderness and cut off Lee's army or fight them in the open. Lee stopped the Federals' advance but was unable to beat them.

The Federals faced a decision: retreat or redeploy. In the past, the Federal army in Virginia had always retreated after defeat. This Federal army, under the direction of Lieutenant General Ulysses S. Grant, chose to redeploy and moved off to the east in an attempt to get between Lee and the Confederate capital. Lee's army beat the Federals to the road junction at Spotsylvania Court House and immediately threw up formidable earthworks. On the evening of May 10, the Federals launched an attack against a portion of those works held by Dole's Georgia Brigade. The attack successfully broke through the Confederate line, and the Federals sought to widen their breach. One of the regiments they turned upon was the 32nd North Carolina of Daniel's brigade. Colonel Edmund Brabble was killed in the fighting. Soon, General Lee was rushing brigades up from other positions to drive the Federals out.

Some of those were Tar Heel brigades, including that of Stephen Ramsuer. General Lee sought to advance with Ramsuer's men until the Tar Heels took hold of Lee's horse and forced him to the rear. In the end, the Federals were pushed back over the Confederate works with significant losses in a battle that lasted an hour and a half. The Federal army spent May 11 organizing for an even larger attack. Instead of twelve regiments, an entire corps would be used. General Lee was uncertain of the Federal plans and thought they were moving toward Fredericksburg.

On the evening of May 11–12, Lee, with intentions of sliding east, removed the artillery inside the Confederate position known as the Mule Shoe. At 4:35 a.m., the Federals attacked. Due to several factors—the absence of artillery, damp air fouling the rifled muskets and massed Federal attackers—the Confederate line quickly gave way. To the right and left of the breakthrough, Confederate regiments peeled back and faced the foe, firing so fast that, according to Major Cyrus Watson of the 45th North Carolina, "it was more than human flesh could stand and it was impossible for them to reach our lines." The 45th Regiment was a part of Daniels's Tar Heel brigade and was on the left of the breakthrough. On the right was another Tar Heel brigade under James Lane, which likewise bent back and fired into the Federals. Other Confederate brigades soon counterattacked. Johnston's Tar Heels surged toward the breach. Johnston was struck, and command fell upon Colonel Thomas Garrett of the 5th North Carolina, until he was killed and command passed to Colonel Thomas Toon of the 20th North Carolina. Ramseur's Tar Heel brigade then entered the fray, charging "into the very jaws of death." Ramseur was wounded, and command passed to Colonel Bryan Grimes of the 4th North Carolina. These Tar Heels were able to drive the Federals from portions of their captured works. Other Confederate soldiers arrived, and the Federals fell back over the Confederate works. The Federals were on one side, with the Confederates on the other. It was instant death to rise up and look over, so the armies soon reached a stalemate. Later that day, in an effort to get the stalled Federal advance going, Grant launched a new attack, sending portions of the Ninth Corps at the Confederates to the south of the Mule Shoe against a position later dubbed Heth's Salient. About the same time, Lee sent Lane's brigade and a Virginia brigade on a sweeping maneuver to capture some Federal artillery. Lane's brigade swept past the artillery and plowed into the flank of the attacking column, capturing four Federal flags and numerous prisoners. Colonel William Barber of the 37th North Carolina was captured during the assault. While Lane was unable to bring off the artillery, the Federal attack was stopped. Lee built a new defensive line across the base of the Mule Shoe, and on the evening of May 12, the Confederates abandoned the salient and occupied the new line of works. Tar Heel brigade commander Junius Daniel was mortally wounded during the day, dying on May 13.

While the battle of Spotsylvania Court House was raging in the rain, Federal cavalry in Virginia was battling J.E.B. Stuart's command at Yellow Tavern. During the fighting, Stuart was mortally wounded, along with North Carolina's Brigadier General James B. Gordon, commanding a brigade composed of the 1st, 2nd and 5th Cavalry Regiments. Stuart died on May 12 and was buried in Richmond. Gordon died on May 18 and was interred in Wilkes County, North Carolina.

Lee's and Grant's forces continued to man the trenches around Spotsylvania, with occasional sorties until May 21, when the Federals began moving east once again. And, once again, the Confederates were able to beat the Federals to their next objective: the bridges over the North Anna River near Hanover Junction. The Federals were able to force their way across two points of the river: Chesterfield Bridge and Jericho Mills. However, the two points were separated by the river itself, and the attacking Federal columns could only support one another by re-crossing the river, twice. Cadmus Wilcox's division was chosen to attack the Federals at the Jericho Mills crossing. Wilcox's division contained four brigades, including the Tar Heel brigades of Scales and Lane. While the attack succeeded in pushing the Federals back, reinforcements soon arrived and forced the Confederates to retire. Lee, who was ill during this portion of the campaign, bitterly complained to Wilcox's corps commander, A.P. Hill: "Why did you not do as Jackson would have done, thrown your whole force upon these people and driven them back?" The Battle of Jericho Mills was the most serious engagement in four days of fighting.

Yet again Grant sought to get beyond the Confederate right flank, and yet again Lee's army arrived at Cold Harbor and entrenched before the Federals arrived. Grant believed that Lee's army was at its breaking point, and Grant had run out of maneuvering room this side of the James River. Grant chose to launch an assault on the Confederate line that was over six miles in length early on the morning of June 3. A portion of the Federal force was able to penetrate the Confederate lines, but quick action by the 66th North Carolina of Martin's brigade, only recently transferred to Lee's army, was able to help drive the Federals back. Elsewhere along the lines, the Federals were not able to get close to the Confederate entrenchments. Lee's nearly defeated army had dealt the Federals a stunning defeat, and about

3,500 Federals were killed or wounded on June 3 alone. All told, in forty days of fighting and maneuvering, Grant had lost about 55,000 men, compared with about 33,000 Confederates. For the next few days, the armies above Richmond were stationary, with Grant trying to formulate a new plan while Lee watched and waited for an opportunity to strike.

While Lee's and Grant's armies battled in Virginia, the principal armies in Georgia were also clashing. The Federal force was commanded by William Sherman, while the Confederate Army of Tennessee was under the command of Joseph Johnston. Campaigning began on May 8, just north of the town of Dalton. The Federals pounded away at Confederate defenses on Rocky Face Ridge and at Buzzard's Roost but were unable to dislodge the Confederates. Sherman had already sent a force beyond the Confederate flank, and Johnston was forced to withdraw on May 12 to counter the Federals to his south at Resaca. The Confederate line at Resaca was in the shape of a fishhook, about four miles long. On the morning of May 14, Sherman launched an attack that was beaten back, and the Confederates countered that afternoon with an attack that included the 58th and 60th North Carolina Regiments, which successfully captured the Federal entrenchments. The 58th Regiment, part of Reynolds's brigade, was engaged again on May 15, unsuccessfully charging the Federal lines about dusk. Total losses for these two regiments were seven killed, thirty-six wounded and eighteen captured, with total Confederate losses around three thousand compared to four thousand Federals. The Confederates, attempting to protect their lines of supply and communication, pulled out of their works that evening and headed south. Johnston's army finally settled into a position near Allatoona Pass. Sherman sought to move around the Confederate flank, but Johnston beat him and went into position near New Hope Church. The Federals launched several assaults on May 25 but were unable to drive off the Confederates. On May 27, the Federals attacked at Pickett's Mill but were also unsuccessful. The Tar Heels of Reynolds's brigade were not involved in these actions, but Reynolds was wounded and replaced by Colonel Robert Trigg.

June 1 brought another retreat by a victorious Confederate army. Sherman was again cutting the Confederate railroad, and Johnston had to retreat. Johnston's new line was at Kennesaw Mountain. The Federals attempted to work around the Confederate flank but were thwarted by an attack by the corps of Lieutenant General John B. Hood on June 19. Both the 58th and 60th Regiments were involved in the attack, which failed to drive the Federals back. After charging through an open field against a fortified Federal line with ample artillery, the Tar Heel infantry reported losses of fifteen killed, seventy-six wounded, twenty-one captured and seven missing in action. Sherman, believing that the Confederate forces were overextended, attacked the entrenched lines on Kennesaw on June 27. Sherman suffered one of the biggest losses of the campaign, losing over three thousand men, compared to the one thousand felled Confederates. Not until July 2 did the roads clear enough for Sherman to maneuver again, and for the next few days, the armies were involved in minor skirmishes. The 58th and 60th Regiments rotated on and off duty for the next couple of weeks, and by mid-July they were in the works outside Atlanta.

On July 18, President Davis replaced Johnston as commander of the Army of Tennessee with Hood. Almost immediately, Hood launched a series of attacks, trying to destroy portions of the Federal army on the outskirts of Atlanta. Neither the 58th nor the 60th Regiment appears to have been involved in these battles; for much of the battle and siege to reduce Atlanta, they were manning the works around the city. In late August, the Tar Heel regiments caught up with their division. At the same time,

David Young served as a lieutenant in the 29th North Carolina Troops until elected to the House of Commons in 1862. His Mitchell County home was raided toward the end of the war. *Robert Morgan.*

Reynolds's old brigade was consolidated with Brown's brigade and placed under the command of Brigadier General Joseph Palmer. Hood sent the soldiers south of Atlanta to Jonesborough to counter what turned out to be more than just a raid against the railroad. Sherman had moved almost his entire army to cut Atlanta's last rail connection. The Confederate attacks were uncoordinated and unsuccessful, and by the first of September, Hood was forced to abandon Atlanta. Hood then took his army north, cutting Sherman's supply lines and almost taking Allatoona Pass. The 29th and portions of the 39th North Carolina Regiments, which had been reassigned to the Army of Tennessee, helped capture a portion of the Federal lines before the threat of reinforcements forced the Confederates to withdraw. Major Ezekiel Hampton reported that the 29th Regiment lost twelve killed, thirty-nine wounded and three missing.

Hood continued moving north, tearing up the tracks and looking for a way to attack a portion of Johnston's command. By late October, Hood was in Alabama, and on November 2, he began crossing the Tennessee River into Tennessee. Columbia, Tennessee, fell on November 27, and the 58th North Carolina was left to garrison the town and guard prisoners as the rest of the army moved north. The Federal army slipped by the sleeping Confederates at Spring Hill, en route to Franklin. A lack of bridges over the Harpeth River prevented the Federals from crossing, and they chose to entrench in front of the town. Hood sent his men forward in one of the bloodiest assaults of the war. While the Confederates were able to break the Federal lines around the Carter House, they were eventually repulsed, losing almost seven thousand men, including six slain generals. None of the Tar Heel regiments in the Army of Tennessee was present during the battle. The Federal army slipped over the river on November 30, after fighting the battle, and retreated to Nashville, where they joined other elements of the Federal army in Tennessee. Hood continued to follow but chose not to assault the superior force in Nashville, choosing instead to have his army entrench, an invitation for Federal attack. On December 2, the two brigades were sent from Nashville to reinforce a scouting expedition to Murfreesboro led by famed Confederate cavalry commander Nathan Bedford Forrest. This included Palmer's brigade and the 60th North Carolina. On December 6, Forrest reconnoitered the Murfreesboro defenses and then fell back and dug in when the Federals launched their own reconnaissance. The Federal attack on December 7 pushed back the Confederates. Lieutenant Colonel James T. Weaver, commanding the 60th Regiment, was killed in the fighting. The 60th Regiment continued to operate away from the main army, tearing up

Lieutenant Colonel James T. Weaver, 60th North Carolina Troops, was killed at the Battle of Murfreesboro, Tennessee, in December 1864. *Library of Congress.*

railroads and posing a threat to the Federals in Murfreesboro, only rejoining the army on December 18.

Orders came for the 58th North Carolina, stationed at Columbia, on December 12: cook rations and prepare to move about 1,200 prisoners to Mississippi. The expedition moved out on December 14, arriving between December 22 and 23. The 58th Regiment moved farther west in response to a Federal raid at the end of the month and did not rejoin the Army of Tennessee until mid-January 1865.

The reinforced Federals in Nashville, about seventy thousand soldiers, took Hood up on his offer of battle and attacked the Confederate lines on December 15. Hood had about twenty-one thousand men. The Federals launched a diversionary attack on the Confederate right before striking and overwhelming the Confederate left. Ector's brigade, with the 29th and 39th Regiments, was posted on the Confederate left, and when the Federals advanced, they fell back, closer to Hood's main battle lines, near redoubt No. 5. This position was also untenable, as Hood's force withdrew. Ector's brigade of Texans and Carolinians fell back to Brentwood Hills and successfully stymied a small Federal attack that evening. During the night, Hood designated a new defensive line, hoping the Federals would attack. This new line was located on a series of hills that Ector's brigade already occupied. Hood's soldiers dressed to the right of Ector's current position and dug in. Surprisingly, Ector's late stand against a Federal cavalry regiment caused dread to ripple through the Federal high command, which believed that the Confederates were massing for a flank attack. Ector was later pulled back into a supporting position and, on December 16, sent to once again help Confederate cavalry attempting to protect the Confederate rear. Hood pulled so many men out of the trench that when the Federals finally did attack, there were not enough defenders to resist the attack and the Confederate line gave way. It is possible that Ector's brigade was one of two brigades that helped keep open the line of Confederate retreat.

The remnants of the Army of Tennessee were forced to retreat. Ector's brigade, under the command of Colonel David Coleman of the 39th Regiment, was one of eight infantry brigades used by Nathan Bedford Forrest to protect the rear of the Confederate column and was perhaps the last of the Confederate infantry over the Tennessee River. The remnants of the Army of Tennessee moved back into north Alabama to rest and refit, and on January 13, Hood requested to be reassigned to another post and was subsequently relieved of command.

In Virginia, Grant had run out of options in trying to get between Lee's army and Richmond. Just a few days after the disastrous assault at Cold Harbor, Grant began secretly moving a portion of his army south of the James River, with plans to capture the important railroad hub at Petersburg, hoping to cut the supplies coming into the city. The area was under the direct command of Confederate general P.G.T. Beauregard. Under Federal pressure, Beauregard abandoned the defensives at Bermuda Hundred on June 15. The defenders, the division of Robert F. Hoke, including the Tar Heel brigade of Thomas Clingman, were moved to the Petersburg defenses but quickly abandoned the outer Petersburg works and fell back closer to Petersburg, constructing new works. On June 16, Beauregard's force had grown from 2,200 men to 10,000 men, and they were facing, according to Beauregard, 66,000 Federal soldiers. Beauregard then ordered Bushrod Johnson's brigade to abandon the Bermuda Hundred line and report to Petersburg. Johnson's division contained Ransom's Tar Heel brigade, commanded by Colonel Leroy McAfee of the 49th North Carolina. About 5:00 p.m., the Federals attacked, continuing their assault until 11:00 p.m. Once they broke through the Confederate lines, but Johnson's division began to arrive and pushed the Federals back. That evening, Beauregard created a third line of defense, and his men once again fell back and entrenched. New attacks began at dawn and continued throughout June 17. Late that day, a Federal attack breached a section of the Confederate line, and Brigadier General Matt Ransom's brigade was among the Confederates rushed to shore up that section of the Confederate line. The 35th North Carolina found itself engaged in hand-to-hand combat in the trenches, and Colonel John Jones was struck three different times and killed. Lee had finally realized that the bulk of the Federal army had been transferred to the Petersburg front, and he quickly began sending Beauregard reinforcements, which started to arrive on June 18.

The siege of Petersburg was now underway, and Robert E. Lee believed that it was only "a matter of time" before he would be forced to capitulate. The Federals tried many different tactics to root Lee from his entrenchments: raids to cut the railroads, which were often repaired; attacks north of the river; and even a mine dug and detonated under Confederate lines. Early on the morning of July 30, 1864, a mine that took weeks to dig under Confederate entrenchments was lit, exploding just to the left of Ransom's brigade. Even before the dirt and dust settled, the Federal soldiers were rushing toward the hole in the Confederate line, yelling, "No quarter to the Rebels!" Alas, it was the Federals who received no quarter. Once the Federal soldiers reached the crater, order broke down and they were unable to advance. Federal reserves arrived, including members of the United States Colored Troops, which only compounded the problem. Confederates lined the rim of the crater, pouring a destructive fire into the troops below. As more Confederate reinforcements arrived, they charged into the crater, with the 25th North Carolina leading the van. Lieutenant Charles Ferguson recalled that "the fight was hand to hand, with guns, bayonets, and swords, in fact anything a man could fight with." The Federals were pushed back, and it is probable that many of the wounded and surrendering black soldiers were killed in the melee.

The Petersburg front was not the only concern of Lee and his army. Just before the battle of the crater, the Federals launched an attack against the Confederate defensives at Deep Bottom, on the James River. Their multifaceted goal was to draw the Confederate raiders down the Shenandoah Valley back into Virginia, reopen the James River to Federal supply trips and, if possible, capture Richmond itself. While the Federals were able to reopen the river to traffic on July 27, they were not successful in their other endeavors. The Confederates attacked the Federal right flank on July 28, but a counterattack caught the 7th North Carolina on the flank and forced Lane's brigade back. As an aside, Lee, fearing a push on Richmond, weakened the Petersburg defenses about the time of the attack on the crater.

With rumors circulating the second week of August 1864 of a Confederate buildup in Northern Virginia, Grant chose to attack along the Richmond-Petersburg lines, hoping to find a weak spot, or at least to draw the Confederates back. Portions of the Army of the Potomac attacked again at Deep Bottom the week of August 14. Numerous Tar Heel regiments were involved in the defense. Ruffus Barringer's cavalry brigade, composed of the 1st, 2nd, 3rd and 5th Regiments, attacked on the morning of August 15, driving the Federals back two miles. On August 16, the Federals attacked again, breaking the line held by a brigade of Georgians. This caused panic in the Tar Heel brigade of James Lane, under the command of Colonel William Barber of the 37th North Carolina, but the Tar Heels rallied. A charge by this brigade and other Confederate commands drove the Federals out of the Confederate entrenchments. Barber was wounded, and command of the brigade passed to Colonel William Speer of the 28th North Carolina.

While fighting north of the James River, Grant launched a raid against the Weldon Railroad below Petersburg. On August 18, the Federals attacked, driving Confederate pickets back to Globe Tavern. Beauregard could spare only three brigades from the Petersburg entrenchments to counter the Federal trust, but those three brigades were able to punch a hole through the Federal line. By the time the Federals had recovered and formed a new line that caused Heth to fall back, Heth's men had caused significant Federal losses, especially by taking prisoners. In the confusion, the flag of the 55th North Carolina was captured by a member of the 56th Pennsylvania Infantry, and Brigadier General Thomas L. Clingman was wounded in the leg. Confederate reinforcements were rushed to the area. Action in the area heated up again on August 21, but the Confederates were unable to penetrate the new Federal entrenchments. A member of the 11th Pennsylvania Infantry captured the flag of the 24th North Carolina.

It was the Federals' hope to visit even more destruction on the Weldon Railroad, and additional troops were ordered to the area. By the evening of August 24, eight more miles of tracks had been destroyed, and a Federal corps lay bivouacked at Reams Station. General Lee threw A.P. Hill's entire corps, some thirty-eight regiments, nineteen of which consisted of Tar Heels, at the lightly entrenched Federal position. The Tar Heels routed the Federals, capturing over two thousand men in the attack, along with nine pieces of artillery and twelve flags. That evening, the Federals were forced to retreat closer to the Union lines. Northern morale dropped to its lowest point of the war following Reams Stations, and Lincoln feared he would lose his bid for reelection in November. However, the loss of so much of the Weldon Railroad crippled the Confederate supply system.

Fighting again broke out at the end of September. The Federals launched September 28 attacks on both the Richmond and Petersburg fronts, which met with success and the loss of Fort Harrison. The Confederates valiantly tried to recapture the works on September 30, but Tar Heels in Clingman's and Martin's brigades, along with Hagood's South Carolinians and Colquitt's Georgians, attacked in vain. The Federals held the fort. On September 30, the Federals south of Petersburg moved farther west in an attempt to capture the Boydton Plank Road and further cut supplies coming into Petersburg. Lee quickly rushed reinforcements, including some destined for the action at Fort Harrison, into the area. The Confederates, many of them Tar Heels in the brigades of Lane and McRae, attacked, driving the Federals from two different positions. Federal reinforcements and overwhelming artillery support eventually checked the Confederate advance. Colonel William Barber of the 37th North Carolina received his sixth and final wound in the attack, dying in Petersburg on October 3. Confederate attacks on October 1 produced no notable results, save more causalities. After a disjointed Confederate attack to the east of Richmond along the Darbytown Road, Lee put aside offensive operations for a while.

For some time, Lee had been fighting on more than just two fronts. He had ordered large portions of the Second Corps, Stonewall Jackson's old command, to the Shenandoah Valley. Grant had responded in July by sending troops away from the Petersburg-Richmond front to counter the movements of these Confederates. Once Grant had even started preparations to drastically reduce the number of Federal soldiers at Petersburg to confront the Confederates coming out of the valley. The Valley Campaign produced numerous memorable events. Chambersburg, Pennsylvania, was burned; Washington was threatened; and battles were fought at Monocacy, Snicker's Gap and third Winchester. At the last, fought on September 19, the flag of the 4th North Carolina State Troops was captured by a member of the 1st West Virginia Cavalry. A month later, Confederate corps commander Jubal Early launched an attack on the Federals at Cedar Creek. The Federals were caught by surprise and pushed back a considerable distance. However, the numerically superior Federals were able to regroup and, at the end of the day, pushed the Confederates back. North Carolina native General Stephen D. Ramseur, who had just learned of the birth of his first child, was mortally wounded during the final Federal attack, and the battle flag of the 12th North Carolina State Troops was captured. The divisions that

Early commanded returned to the main Confederate army, and the Valley Campaign slowed to a crawl.

Believing that Lee had severely cut his forces around Petersburg and Richmond, Grant chose to renew his attack in late October. The Federals advanced toward a portion of the Confederate works outside Richmond, near Fair Oaks and Burgess Mill. The initial Confederate attack on October 27 met with success, capturing men and artillery. But hidden Federal infantry counterattacked, and McRae's North Carolina brigade was hard hit, losing six hundred men and the flags from the 26th and 47th Regiments. While victorious, the Federals elected to fall back that evening, leaving the Confederates with numerous prisoners.

Following Burgess Mill, the Tar Heels in the Army of Northern Virginia settled into life in the trenches. Every few days, they rotated on and off picket duty, almost always after dark. Every so often they were called upon to go and defend some other point, and in December, some of them were involved in chasing the Federals raiding toward Jarrett's Station. With the loss of the port of Wilmington in North Carolina, and the destruction of the railroads in Virginia, Lee realized that he needed to get his command out of the trenches around Petersburg and Richmond and link up with Joseph Johnston's army in North Carolina. On March 25, Lee launched an attack on Fort Stedman. If the attack succeeded, Grant would be forced to withdraw a portion of his left, making the Confederate escape toward North Carolina easier. Like so many other Confederate operations during the siege of Petersburg, the Confederate attack initially met with success: a portion of the Federal line was captured. But the Federal reinforcements had arrived, and the Confederates were forced to withdraw. This setback was followed by the ninth and last offensive launch by Grant during the Petersburg campaign. The Federals captured Dinwiddie Court House on March 29. This was to the right of the main Confederate line and threatened the railroads that ran from the west into Petersburg. Lee began to shift portions of his army farther right to counter the Federal advance. The Confederates reached the important Five Forks junction first. Yet again the Confederate attacks met with success, pushing the Federals back on March 31. During the night, the Confederate commander in charge of operations at Five Forks, George Pickett, chose to retreat back to Five Forks. On April 1, the Federals attacked and were able to drive the Confederates away.

Knowing that Lee had pulled Confederate soldiers from other points along his line to deal with the threat at Five Forks, Grant ordered an all-out assault for the morning of April 2. Grant later scaled this attack back to two points:

The 37th North Carolina Troops received this flag in November–December 1862. The lettering was distinctive to the regiments of the Branch-Lane brigade. *Museum of the Confederacy*.

one corps would attack Fort Mahone along the Jerusalem Plank Road while another corps struck the Confederate line between Petersburg and Hatcher's Run. Following a nearly all-night bombardment meant to weaken the Confederate lines, the Federals stepped out a little after 4:00 a.m. While the corps that attacked along the Jerusalem Plank Road bogged down, the other attack met with success. These lines were held by four regiments of Lane's brigade: the 18th, 28th, 33rd and 37th North Carolina Troops. The 7th Regiment of Lane's Brigade had been sent back to North Carolina a few weeks before. According to one of Lane's Tar Heels, the men were some five feet apart, trying to cover ground normally held by two or three brigades. In the twenty-minute hand-to-hand fight, where rifles, swords and bayonets were freely used, the Federals were able to break through the Confederate lines. In the melee, the flag of the 37th North Carolina was captured, and A.P. Hill was killed in the ensuing confusion. As the Federals entered the works, they sent troops to both the right and left to take the Confederate lines by the flank. Some of the Tar Heels from Lane's brigade, along with men from Mississippi and Louisiana, about three hundred soldiers total, retreated into Batteries Gregg and Whitworth. After several bloody attempts, five thousand Federal soldiers were able to capture Battery Gregg, forcing the Confederates to withdraw from Whitworth. Elsewhere, the Federals were able to make inroads in the Confederate works, but some defenders still held the Federals at bay.

Later that afternoon, Lee ordered the withdrawal of the Confederate soldiers from the breastworks around Petersburg and Richmond, which began at 10:00 p.m. Civilian authorities loaded the important papers of the Confederate government onto train cars and then boarded themselves for a hasty getaway. Fires were set to military stores and warehouses in the city, and looters roamed the streets. Grant ordered a charge for the morning of April 3 but quickly discovered that all the able-bodied Confederate soldiers were gone. Petersburg was soon in Federal hands, and then Richmond followed. The very first Federal troops to enter Richmond were the 36th United States Colored Troops, formerly known as the 2nd North Carolina Colored Troops. At one point during their advance, they were ordered to the side of the road so that white troops could pass them and obtain that honor. The 36th did move to the side of the road but did not stop advancing, much to the chagrin of the white regiments. The stay of the black regiments was short, and by April 12, they had been relocated outside Richmond.

Amelia Court House, to the west of Petersburg and Richmond, was the rendezvous point for the retreating Confederates. General William Robert's

The 36th United States Colored Troops, formerly known as the 2nd North Carolina Colored Volunteers, was the first regiment to enter Richmond after Confederate evacuation. *From Harper's Weekly.*

cavalry brigade, composed of the 4th North Carolina Cavalry and the 16th North Carolina Cavalry Battalion, served as the rear guard for some of the retreating Confederates. They skirmished with the Federals at Namozine Creek and were forced back. The Tar Heel brigade of Brigadier General Rufus Barringer replaced Roberts, and Barringer's brigade skirmished with the Federals at Namozine Church. The flag of the 2nd North Carolina Cavalry, along with Barringer and his staff, was captured.

As Lee was in the process of evacuating his works, he ordered 350,000 rations sent by train to Amelia Court House. However, when the army arrived, the men found ordnance stores instead of subsistence. Lee sent out a plea to people living in the area, along with wagons to forage for provisions. "This delay was fatal and could not be retrieved," Lee later remarked as the wagons returned nearly empty. By early afternoon, the army was again moving west, but irreplaceable time had been lost. When Federals blocked their path toward North Carolina near Burkeville, the Confederates chose to continue farther west toward Farmville, hoping to pass the Federal flank and turn south. Numerous rearguard actions were fought as the Confederates worked their way west. Some, like the April 6 action at High Bridge, were stunning Confederate victories. Another action fought on that same day, the Battle of Sailor's Creek, is considered the darkest day in the history of the Army of Northern Virginia. At the latter, a portion of the Confederate army became separated from the main body and was attacked by the Federals. The Confederate force fought gallantly, and at one point, a portion counterattacked and drove the Federals back across the creek. But overwhelming Federal numbers soon surrounded most of the Confederate force, and almost eight thousand Confederates, along with six generals, were compelled to surrender. The flags of the 4th, 6th and 21st Regiments were taken as trophies that day. Many believe the Battle of Sailor's Creek to be the deathblow to Lee's army.

The remnants of the Army of Northern Virginia trudged toward the west, with countless men abandoning the army as it marched. On April 7, Grant sent Lee a letter asking Lee to avoid further "effusion of blood" by surrendering "that portion of the C.S. Army known as the Army of Northern Virginia." Lee responded by asking Grant for the terms of surrender. Portions of the armies fought again on April 8 at Appomattox Station, with the Federals once again victorious. Missives between Lee and Grant continued to be traded as Lee's army arrived on the outskirts of Appomattox Court House. Plans were laid by the Confederates for battle on the morning of April 9 to cut through the Federal cavalry and continue south. Early that next morning, the Confederate infantry attacked, capturing two pieces of artillery and pushing back the cavalry. However, the Federal cavalry held long enough for the infantry to arrive, and the opportunity was lost. In the action that morning, Sergeant Ivy Ritchie of the 14th North Carolina State Troops was struck and killed, the final soldier in the Army of Northern Virginia to die fighting. White flags soon went out from the Confederate lines, and a cease-fire went into effect. Lee met with Grant at the McLean home in Appomattox, and later that afternoon, Lee surrendered the Army of Northern Virginia. "The life of the C.S. is gone," wrote one member of the 37th North Carolina. On April 10 and 11, the cavalry and artillery were paroled. On April 12, the Confederate infantry marched between two lines of Federal infantry, stacked arms, furled the colors and marched off to receive passes and parolees. Of the 27,549 men surrendered by General Lee, 4,871 were from North Carolina. Of the flags surrendered that day, only that of the 28th North Carolina is attributed to that period of time. The others were already lost, were destroyed by the men or were secreted home. Lieutenant William Blanton of the 38th North Carolina recalled after the war that on the surrender, "I had never seen before nor since such shaking of hands, such shedding of tears, such crying aloud, such rushing of the soldiers to get hold of Lee's hand, never has been witnessed, and the General had a kind word for all—with tears streaming from his eyes." The Tar Heels of the Army of Northern Virginia pocketed their paroles and started walking toward the Old North State.

Chapter 7
Reconstruction

As the veterans of the Army of Tennessee mingled with those returning from the Army of Northern Virginia, they returned to a state torn asunder by four years of war. The Federal army had occupied much of the eastern portions of the state for the duration of the conflict. In the western counties, guerrilla war and anarchy had ruled the day, and portions of the central counties, much of the breadbasket of the state, also had endured inner-civil war. Families had turned on families, and even brothers on brothers. Added to this, a large mounted army had scoured the western half of the state, while two different Federal armies had marched through the eastern portions, one from New Bern to Goldsboro and the other via Fayetteville to Raleigh. As the Confederate armies were disbanded, the former soldiers returned to a land that was deeply torn and, in many places, utterly uninhabitable. Businesses and farms had fallen to fire, and fields were fallow.

Furthermore, the soldiers returned to a state that had no civil government and was under the command of the United States military. William T. Sherman officially placed Major General John Schofield in command of the Department of North Carolina when he left for Washington, D.C., on April 28, 1865. Just a day prior to that, Schofield had issued a general order stating that the war in North Carolina had come to an end and that it was "now the duty of all to cultivate friendly relations with the same zeal which has characterized our conduct of the war." On May 1, as paroles were being issued to the soldiers of the Army of Tennessee, Governor Vance

Major General John Schofield (U.S.) declared in April 1865 that the war in North Carolina was over. *Library of Congress.*

met with Schofield, learning that all elected officials no longer held power. Vance, unsure of his status, attempted to surrender to Schofield, who had no orders for Vance's imprisonment. Vance traveled to Statesville where his family waited.

Had the war simply ended in April and May 1865, with the surrenders of Lee and Johnston and the capture of Davis, the former soldiers might have merely returned and started rebuilding their lives. However, lawlessness plagued the state. In the western portions of North Carolina, guerrilla bands roamed freely. The Adair gang ran roughshod over Rutherford County, robbing, plundering and even killing members of a black family seeking to protect themselves. Things were little better in Wilkes County, where a gang occupied a local house. The group terrorized residents in three or four adjacent counties. Several attempts were made by locals to rout the men from their stronghold, known as Fort Hamby. Finally, a group of former Confederate soldiers, possibly numbering "several hundred men," attacked the fort, eventually setting fire to the log structure. The renegades surrendered and were executed on the spot. Sometimes, bandits were operating independently. A Federal deserter who was arrested in Asheville while trying to steal the horse of the colonel of the 5th Ohio Cavalry claimed to have killed nineteen Tar Heels since the war ended. The eastern part of the state was little better. In May, members of the 1st USCT skirmished with a band of mounted guerrillas in Sampson County. Only the presence of large numbers of Federal soldiers kept events from getting worse. In early May 1865, there were forty-six thousand Federal soldiers in North Carolina, but the bulk of Sherman's army had already headed north to participate in the Grand Review held in Washington, D.C., on May 23 and 24.

On May 13, Governor Vance was arrested and sent to old Capital Prison in Washington, D.C., where he shared a cell with five others, including the former governors of Georgia and Virginia, Joseph Brown and John Letcher. Forty-seven days after his arrest, Vance, who was never charged, was released on parole and allowed to return home.

President Andrew Johnson issued two proclamations on May 29 regarding the policies of his presidential Reconstruction. The first concerned all the former Confederate states. Amnesty was granted to all former Confederates, except those who fell into fourteen classes. Some of those exemptions included those who had attained the rank of colonel or above, persons who had more than $20,000, ex-governors and those who were officials of the Confederate government. These men were able to write to the president, via their local governors, and request a presidential pardon. Johnson's second proclamation installed former Vance supporter and peace party leader William Holden as governor of North Carolina and restored the authority and function of Federal law, tax and custom collections. Holden had several colossal tasks: to fill all local and state-level positions with loyal men and to call for a convention to amend the state constitution. To vote for delegates to the convention, a man both had to take the amnesty oath and be qualified per the state constitution as of May 1, 1861. The latter disallowed any non-whites from voting on delegates. In August 1865, Holden called for an election of delegates in September to meet in Raleigh in October. The convention abolished slavery and nullified the secession ordinance, but when it came to repudiating the state's war debt, almost $19 million, the conventioneers reached an impasse. Repudiating the debt meant the loss of most of the state's assets and credit, along with loss to private holders of

William Holden was
appointed governor
of North Carolina in
1865, voted out of
office, reelected in 1867,
impeached in 1868
and then pardoned in
2011. *North Carolina State
Archives.*

the state's bonds. A note from President Johnson demanding the refutation
of the sum broke the impasse, and the convention adjourned, with elections
set for November. State Treasurer Jonathan Worth defeated Holden for the
position of governor in North Carolina, but Holden supporters won four
out of seven congressional seats and the majority in the General Assembly.
However, the election demonstrated to President Johnson and, more
importantly, to the radicals in Congress that North Carolina had failed to
create a new political leadership and that the prewar, slave-owning class still
maintained power. "There seems, in many of the elections, something like
defiance, which is all out of place at this time," Johnson wrote.

Violence was still rampant across the state. In Raleigh, Federal soldiers
robbed black-owned stores and beat their proprietors, and at the same
time, black Union soldiers and white Union soldiers clashed in the streets.
On Roanoke Island, white soldiers stole from black citizens, and when
the freedmen complained, the freedmen were jailed. On election day in
September, a large group of freed people was meeting in Concord, listening
to a speaker from the Freedmen's Bureau, when they were attacked by a
group of white men. The local officials were forced to call upon the military
for help, and the ringleaders were captured and prosecuted. Similar attacks
occurred in Wilkesboro and Salem on July 4, 1866. In Pitt County, armed
and mounted groups calling themselves "Regulators" attacked both white

and black families, while the Federal army skirmished with the same groups in Pitt and Lenoir Counties.

This is not to say that all of the violence was directed against freed people. The newspapers of the time are filled with stories of gangs of black men who raided white farms. A group of five such men attacked the home of Mr. Berry in Jones County, taking firearms, jewelry, food and livestock and assaulting the people inside. According to a Harrisburg, Pennsylvania newspaper article, the occupants were tied up and left inside as the attackers attempted to burn the house down. In Morganton, recently mustered-out black Union troops, who had joined with Stoneman as he rode through the area, came to the town and were so "insolent" that the white troops stationed there drove them out. In early 1866, Craven County citizens sent Governor Worth a letter asking for protection from the gangs of freedmen who were terrorizing locals. At Wilmington, a corporal and three privates of the 37th USCT were tried for the murder of a white citizen. In 1868, black Federal soldiers led a riot in Smithville. There were even rumors that freedmen of Martin County planned to burn the town of Wilmington.

While the number of Federal troops in North Carolina had fallen drastically, there were still soldiers spread out across the state at different posts. In December 1865, there were 2,209 troops in North Carolina, a 95 percent reduction over the previous six months. These troops were posted in different cities and towns in North Carolina, from Fort Macon on the coast, which served as a prison, to Morganton and Asheville. At some of these posts, the soldiers got along well with the local civilian population. Major General Jacob D. Cox, who replaced Schofield in June 1865, was praised as a "most courteous and elegant man." At other times, the soldiers caused many problems for the locals. Governor Holden was informed that the garrison in Morganton had "become a terror" to the local citizens, "robbing and plundering both white and black." One problem might have been the constant turnover of commanders. Cox was soon replaced by Brigadier General Thomas Ruger. One year later, Ruger was replaced by Brigadier General John Robinson, who served until May 1866, when he was replaced by Major General Daniel Sickles.

In an effort to manage the large number of refugees created by the war, the Bureau of Refugees, Freedmen and Abandoned Lands, better known as the Freedmen's Bureau, was created by Congress in March 1865. The mission of the Freedmen's Bureau was to help those displaced and impoverished by the war, to protect freedmen from injustice, to encourage education and to help freedmen find jobs and receive fair wages. It was

Major General
Daniel Sickles (U.S.)
became commander
of North Carolina
during congressional
Reconstruction. *Library of
Congress*.

not until June 1865 that a bureau agent, Colonel Eliphalet Whittlesey, was assigned to North Carolina. Whittlesey divided the state into four districts, with assistant superintendents in charge. In many instances, Whittlesey used army personnel to staff the different posts in the state. This led to many problems, as the size of the military force in North Carolina was constantly changing. Many in North Carolina were opposed to the Freedmen's Bureau. Catherine Ann Edmondston, writing from her home in Halifax County, believed that the bureau was a nuisance: "No sooner are the negroes seemingly content & beginning to work steadily than some Major, Capt, or Lieut in the Free negro service with more time than brains announces a Speech to the Freedmon in Halifax, when 'down goes the shovel & hoe' and presto away they all start to drink some new draught from the 'Free Spring,' & they come home with their heads filled with their fancied rights…that discipline & and order are at an end for days." In May 1866, Whittlesey and ten other North Carolina bureau officials were relieved by the War

Department, placed under arrest and charged with embezzlement and criminal neglect. From that point until the bureau closed in May 1869, the Federal military commander of North Carolina also served as the commander of the Freedmen's Bureau in North Carolina.

The General Assembly passed a set of "Black Codes" in January 1866, an effort to define the rights of the recently emancipated slaves. North Carolina's codes were considered some of the most liberal in the South. While the laws did not grant citizenship to freed people, they did validate marriages of former slaves, changed the apprenticeship law so that it applied equally to everyone and gave freedmen equal rights and privileges concerning courts and trials, including the right to testify in court cases. These Black Codes, passed by Southern states, led Congress to pass the Civil Rights Act of 1866, which granted citizenship to everyone, regardless of race and color, save Native Americans. Furthermore, all citizens had the right to make and enforce contracts; sue and be sued; give evidence in court; and inherit, purchase, lease, sell, hold and convey real and personal property. Also in January 1866, the Congressional Joint Committee on Reconstruction began to investigate the former Confederate states, trying to ascertain if they were entitled to have their elected congressional representatives seated in either house of Congress. Among the 144 questioned were 11 men from North Carolina. It was this committee that drafted what would become the Fourteenth Amendment of the Constitution and required Southern states to ratify the amendment before they could be readmitted to the Union.

On April 2, 1866, President Johnson declared the insurrection over and peace restored in every Southern state but Texas. Nevertheless, North Carolinians continued to struggle in rebuilding their state. There was still the threat of arrest and imprisonment. In February 1866, Major John Gee, former commander at the Salisbury Prison Camp, was tried for mistreating Federal prisoners of war there. After a lengthy trail, Gee was acquitted. There was also talk of trying former Confederate generals George Pickett and Robert Hoke for their roles in the execution of former Confederate soldiers captured near Kinston while in the service of the United States Army. The board responsible for the investigation later ruled that only Pickett was liable, but the Virginian was never formally charged.

In December 1866, the General Assembly passed an Amnesty Act, pardoning civilian and military men for any act of war committed in the state during the war. However, the act failed to pardon civilians who had served as guides, spies or had avoided conscription. Back in May 1865, President Johnson had set up a system offering amnesty to the rank and file, providing that the former soldiers swore an oath to defend the United States and support the laws of the government. There were fourteen exemptions, and men in these classes had to apply for a presidential pardon. These applications had to go through the governor, who recommended to the president which ones should be pardoned. In several cases, Governor Holden withheld his approval and did not forward the pardons to the president. Many felt Holden withheld the pardons of those who were possible threats to his political aspirations. When Holden was defeated for the office of governor, his successor found in the governor's office more than three hundred applications for pardon that had not been acted upon. Some of these were the leading conservatives in the state. Thomas Clingman, who had advocated secession for many years prior to the war, did not receive his pardon until January 1867. Wartime governor Zebulon Vance received his pardon in March 1867 and former governor Henry Clark in July 1867. Once these men were pardoned, they were allowed to move about freely and to run for political office.

Congress continued to pass even more restrictive laws, often over the veto of President Johnson. Finally, Congress determined that presidential Reconstruction was a failure and, in March 1867, instituted the first of its Reconstruction acts. President Johnson's plans for states to gain re-admittance to the Union were set aside. The Southern states, except Tennessee, were divided into five military districts. North and South Carolina were designated as the Second Military District and placed under the command of Major General Daniel Sickles, who was later replaced by Brigadier General Edward Canby. Now, each state was ordered to draft a new constitution, which would need to be submitted to Congress for approval. The new constitution must allow freedmen the right to vote, and the new General Assembly elected under the new constitution must ratify the Fourteen Amendment. Once all of these criteria were met, a state would then be re-admitted to the Union. Jonathan Worth was left as governor of North Carolina but now found his position severely limited since the commander of each district was given totality of power, with the ability to remove state and local officers at his discretion.

Canby ordered elections for a convention to be held on October 18, 1867. Of the 179,653 registered voters, 93,006 voted for the convention, with 32,961 against. Earlier that year, Holden and his supporters had met in Raleigh and organized a statewide Republican Party. In the October election, Holden and the Republicans captured 107 out of the 120 delegate seats at the convention. The convention delegates gathered in Raleigh and

Jonathan Worth served as North Carolina treasurer from 1863 to 1865 and governor from 1865 until 1867. *North Carolina State Archives.*

drafted a document that pulled from both the previous constitutions and from those of other states. Abolishing slavery and providing universal male suffrage were elements of the new document, along with giving the power to men to elect representatives, judges and county officials. The ownership of property was no longer a qualification for voting, and the governor's term was increased from two to four years. A lieutenant governor was added, and he also filled the role of president of the senate. Other changes included electing supreme court judges to eight years, increasing the number of judges from three to five, popular elections of county sheriffs and free public schools for both white and black children. The last Reconstruction act was passed in March 1868, calling for a simple majority of votes cast for a state to ratify the new constitution. The ratification of the new constitution was held simultaneously with a general election, April 21–23. Some claimed that the Republicans brought in black students from Howard University to ensure the constitution's passage. In the end, 93,084 voted for ratification, with 74,015 against. Nearly 30,000 registered voters did not cast a ballot.

William Holden was elected governor, with the Republicans carrying fifty-eight of eighty-nine counties. The conservatives managed to elect only one congressman, one judge and one solicitor. North Carolina was re-admitted to the Union on June 25, 1868, along with Louisiana, Florida and South Carolina. Canby ordered Worth to step down, and on July 1, Holden was sworn in as governor.

Holden called the General Assembly into session, and on July 3, 1868, the new constitution was ratified. On July 6, the United States Congress agreed to admit three of the Tar Heel congressional representatives. On July 24, Canby officially turned over control of the government to state officials, as laid out by the Congressional Acts, and Reconstruction came to an end in North Carolina.

The end of Radical Reconstruction did not effect an end to the war in North Carolina. If anything, the rise of the Republican Party, bringing about North Carolina's readmission to the Union, only escalated hostilities. Wartime secret organizations, like the Heroes of America and the Red Strings, reorganized after the war into Union Leagues, often consisted of both whites and blacks. The purpose of the Union League was to "elect Union men to office and for mutual protection." One man in Alamance County informed Governor Holden that he was willing to fight before letting "unhung rebels" regain political office. And if the letters that Holden received are true, fight they did, usually in a subversive role. News of a conservative secret organization, the Ku Klux Klan, created in western Tennessee in the spring of 1866, filtered into North Carolina, and by late 1867, some North Carolinians had joined the organization. Between 1868 and 1870, membership in the Klan swelled, and by one estimate, it contained forty thousand members. Some of these members took to dressing in elaborate costumes, were heavily armed and rode at night terrorizing white and black Republicans alike. Some Republicans are even rumored to have joined the Klan in an effort to protect their businesses. The alleged leader of the Klan in Yancey County was John H. Ray, a former captain in the Federal army. Klan violence was especially fierce in Alamance, Stokes, Chatham, Orange, Rockingham, Rutherford and Cleveland Counties, as the Klansmen set out to wrest political power away from the liberals. On February 26, 1870, a large group of Klansmen rode to the home of the local Union League president in Graham. Wyatt Outlaw, a black Republican, had helped found the party in North Carolina. Wyatt was taken to the town square and hanged about thirty yards from the Alamance County courthouse. Two months later, Klansmen lured Caswell County Republican state senator John W.

Stephens into a basement room in the courthouse, where he was tied up and stabbed to death. No one was convicted for either offense. Similar violence was repeated throughout many corners of the state. Even though there were Federal troops still stationed in North Carolina, Governor Holden, using a new 1869 law, declared that Alamance and Caswell Counties were in a state of insurrection. Holden declared martial law and set about organizing a state militia to go into those two counties although there were Federal troops present in Alamance County as early as March 1870.

To deal with this problem, Holden created two militia regiments. The first regiment was placed under the command of former Confederate colonel William J. Clarke and contained both white and black men from eastern North Carolina. The second regiment was placed under the command of Tennessean George W. Kirk, former colonel of the Third North Carolina Mounted Infantry. Up to two-thirds of Kirk's command hailed from east Tennessee. A circular in the western part of North Carolina read: "Rally Union Men in defense of your state!…1000 recruits are wanted immediately, to serve six months unless sooner discharged…Recruits will be received at Asheville, Marshall, and Burnsville, North Carolina." Kirk moved his force into the area, arresting prominent men and keeping them confined in his camp with no writ of habeas corpus. The chief justice of North Carolina, Richmond Pearson, directed the governor to issue the writs, but Holden declined to do so. Later the Federal judge in Salisbury ordered most of Kirk's prisoners to be released. The two militia regiments received the pay, uniforms and equipment of regular Federal soldiers and were paid by the State of North Carolina. The commander of the company of Federal soldiers in Yanceyville believed that Kirk's force was "nothing more than an armed mob" and later reported that Kirk had sworn to burn Yanceyville and kill the prisoners and local women and children when the militia left. The commander believed the presence of Federal troops was the only deterrent to the militia.

What became known as the "Kirk-Holden War" came to a sudden conclusion. In the August 1870 election, the conservatives gained six of the seven congressional seats, the attorney general's seat and a two-to-one majority in the state legislature. The Federal government refused to support Holden's claims, and the cases were dropped. Federal troops sent into the area were recalled, and in September, Holden disbanded his militia. That November, Holden rescinded his proclamation regarding the insurrectionist states in Caswell and Alamance Counties.

There was one final act left to be staged in statewide politics. On December 9, 1870, a resolution was introduced into the North Carolina House to impeach

Governor Holden. There were eight charges leveled at Holden. The first was that Holden, in March 1870, had, after declaring a state of insurrection, sent "bodies of armed, desperate, and lawless men, organized and set on foot without authority of law, into said county, and occupy the same by military force and suspend civil authority, and…arrest[ed] many peaceable and law-abiding citizens of said county of Alamance, then and there about their lawful business; and did detain, hold, imprison, harm, beat, and otherwise maltreat and injure many of them." Article IV of the indictment stated that Holden had used the powers of his office to "incite, procure, order, and command one George W. Kirk, and one B.G. Burgen…to assault, seize, detain and imprison and deprived of their liberty and privileges as freeman and citizens of said state." Article V read, in part, that Holden had "unlawfully recruited, armed, and equipped as soldiers, a large number of men, to wit, five hundred men and more, and organized them as an army…[and] placed [them] under the command and control of one George W. Kirk, as colonel." Articles V and VI detailed some of the problems that Kirk and his band caused. Article VII stated that Holden was responsible for the "large sums of money, to-wit: for the sum of seventy thousand dollars and more, and caused and procure…the treasurer of the state, to…pay out of the treasury such said large sums of money to the agent or paymaster" to Kirk and his band. The North Carolina House believed that Holden had committed "a high misdemeanor in office, in violation of the constitution and laws of the state, and of the peace and interests and dignity thereof." On December 19, the state House passed the resolution and articles of impeachment. Holden's trial, held by the state Senate, began on February 2, 1871, and lasted until March 22, 1871. Holden was convicted of six of the eight charges and, by a vote of thirty-six to thirteen, was removed from office. Holden was the first governor removed from office in the United States. He was replaced by Lieutenant Governor Tod R. Caldwell. As a final act, membership in secret organizations was outlawed by the General Assembly.

However, the Holden story does not end in 1871 with his impeachment. In 2011, the senate of the North Carolina General Assembly voted to pardon Holden, stating that he was unjustly removed from office.

As in the rest of the South, Reconstruction was a turbulent affair in North Carolina. For many, a war that for four years consisted of men marching off to distant spots and the occasional letter home telling of death by an enemy's bullet or some seemingly foreign disease was now on the very doorstep of the entire state. Men and women, white and black, lived in fear, not knowing what lurked around the next bend in the road. The failures of Reconstruction lingered for decades in the Old North State.

Chapter 8

Remembrance

L ike much of the South, North Carolina was left devastated by the Civil War. Ships had been sunk, railroads destroyed, farms burned. More than forty thousand husbands, fathers and brothers had perished. Moreover, parts of the Federal army garrisoned the large cities like Charlotte and Raleigh. Thousands of men lay in graves across the state. Some had been killed in skirmishes and battles; others had died of disease in one of the many hospitals across the Tar Heel State.

Scarcely had the guns fallen silent than work to honor the dead began. Sherman's forces were barely out of Fayetteville when a group of ladies, led by Ann Kyle, the wife of a Confederate captain, obtained from the mayor a plot of land in Cross Creek Cemetery. Kyle raised the money to purchase coffins and have graves dug. Soon thereafter, the remains of thirty Confederate soldiers who had died in various places around town were reinterred in the new Confederate section.

Much of the work of gathering the bodies of Confederate soldiers from the spots where they had fallen across the South was assumed by the women of the different Ladies Aid Societies. Following the war, these groups had reorganized themselves into Ladies Memorial Associations. The Ladies Memorial Association of Wake County was organized in May 1866, with Nancy Branch, the widow of General Branch, president. The purpose of the group was to "protect and care for the graves of our Confederate soldiers." Unlike the Soldier Aid Societies that had been solely made up of women, the Ladies Memorial Associations often contained men as well. Among the various committees Branch established was a cemetery committee, made up of three men, charged with exploring suitable sites for a Confederate cemetery and checking on the existing graves of Confederates around Raleigh. One such place was the Rock Quarry Cemetery, near the former Pettigrew Hospital. The hospital was then serving as barracks for Federal soldiers, and the Federal army had began to bury its own dead in the cemetery. The Ladies Memorial Association thought about planting a hedge to separate the graves of North and South but soon settled on the idea of moving the four to five hundred Confederate graves. They approached community leader Henry Mordecia, who donated a plot of ground. Next, the Ladies Memorial Association set about raising funds, cleaning the grounds and disinterring the bodies. In early February 1867, the Ladies Memorial Association petitioned the General Assembly for $1,500 to help with the project, which was granted. However, on February 20, 1867, the Federal commander in Raleigh informed the Ladies Memorial Association that the Confederate graves had to be moved immediately. In the words of one member of the Ladies Memorial Association, written in 1900, if the Confederate remains were not moved quickly, the Federal soldiers would "throw the bodies in the road." The Ladies Memorial Association redoubled its efforts and had the Confederate graves all removed by the end of March 1867.

It was not only the concerned citizens in Raleigh who sought to care for the final resting places of Confederate soldiers. In 1866, a Ladies Memorial Association was organized in Wilmington, and on July 21 of that year, its members decorated the graves of local Confederate soldiers, with an address by Major Joseph Engelhard. The following year, a plot of land in Oakwood Cemetery was donated for the reinterment of 550 soldiers from local hospitals and battlefields. Also in 1866, the Smithville Memorial Association was formed with the purpose of raising funds to erect an iron fence and monument where the Confederate soldiers from the Battle of Averasboro were buried. Ladies Memorial Associations were also organized in New Bern and Charlotte for much the same purpose: to give proper burial to the scores of Confederates who reposed in hastily dug battlefield graves or burial plots near hospitals. In the area near the battlefield of Monroe's Crossroads, the former Confederate soldiers themselves moved the bodies of about thirty Confederate soldiers to the cemetery at Long Street Presbyterian Church.

Though the Ladies Association of Wake County and similar organizations made important contributions to the protection and preservation of Confederate graves, Southerners were not the only ones seeking to gather wartime dead and place them in cemeteries. The Federal government passed

Top row, left to right: Confederate Monument, Cedar Grove Cemetery, New Bern; Confederate Monument, Burnsville. *Bottom row*: Confederate monument, Cross Creek Cemetery, Fayetteville; and Confederate monument, Taylorsville. *Author's collection.*

legislation on April 13, 1866, to find suitable places for the burial of United States soldiers. There were four national cemeteries established in North Carolina. In Salisbury, the government simply took over the grounds that had been used to bury Federal soldiers from the prison camp. The Federal soldiers in Raleigh were already using the cemetery near the Rock Quarry and chose to remove soldiers buried at Averasboro, Smithfield, Bentonville, Goldsboro, Greensboro, Franklin and Henderson. All of the work in Raleigh was finished by the fall of 1867, and a former Federal soldier, G.A. Dichtl, was appointed superintendent in 1868. At New Bern, a portion of ground already containing Federal burials was designated a national cemetery, and soldiers were moved from Beaufort, Morehead, Kingston, Hatteras and Roanoke Island to New Bern. The work of removing and reinterring Federal soldiers in Wilmington was conducted from February to April 1867. Men were brought from the Lutheran and city cemeteries in Wilmington and from Fort Fisher, Smithville, Cape Fear River and along the railroad. In later years, monuments were erected in these national cemeteries, like those placed by Pennsylvania and Maine in the Salisbury Cemetery, commemorating the soldiers from those states.

Not only were graves being cared for, but for Southerners, there was also work on raising appropriate monuments to commemorate Southern dead. After coordinating the movement of Confederate soldiers in Fayetteville, the ladies determined to raise a monument. They pieced together a quilt and began to sell raffle tickets not only in Fayetteville but also in Chapel Hill, Tarboro and Wilmington. Their goal was to raise $1,000. In a war-ravaged economy, they only managed to raise one-third of that sum. Martha Lewis won the quilt in May 1868 and then sent the prize to former Confederate president Jefferson Davis. The ladies next employed a local stonemason to construct and install the monument. On December 30, 1868, the monument to the Confederate dead at Cross Creek Cemetery in Fayetteville, the first in North Carolina, was dedicated. This was the fifth Confederate monument raised in the South following the end of the war.

While it is not clear that a Ladies Memorial Association was involved, a monument was erected over a mass grave of Confederate soldiers at Long Street Presbyterian Church in Cumberland County in 1870. That same year, the Ladies Memorial Association of Wake completed a Confederate monument at Oakwood Cemetery in Raleigh. They had started to raise funds for a simple stone obelisk in 1867 but had met difficulty in the impoverished South. In 1872, the Smithfield Memorial Association complemented the fence they had previously erected at the Chicora Cemetery with a monument. Over a decade would pass before North Carolinians placed another monument.

The Ladies Memorial Associations, while not erecting monuments, were still busy. In the late 1860s, there arose a clamor to return the bodies of Southern soldiers buried at Gettysburg to their respective states. Different Ladies Memorial Associations eventually persuaded Dr. Rufus Weaver of Philadelphia, who had inherited the work of his father, Dr. Samuel Weaver, of Gettysburg, to undertake the work. The senior Weaver had already worked with others in removing the bodies of Union soldiers and prominent Confederate officers for reburial. It took three years to open the graves and identify the remains. When a state could be determined, the remains were sent to that state. A few of the soldiers could be identified by the personal effects that had been left behind. When in doubt, the remains were sent to be reinterred in the soldiers' section of Hollywood Cemetery in Richmond, Virginia. North Carolina's Gettysburg dead were reinterred at the Oakwood Cemetery in Raleigh. All told, there were 143 soldiers reinterred out of 1,600 Tar Heels killed during the battle.

Not only the dead Tar Heels at Gettysburg drew interest. In a memorial service at Oakwood Cemetery in Charlotte in 1883, a speaker lamented that the state's dead at Arlington Cemetery in the District of Columbia were, according to the newspaper, "buried in a corner of the cemetery, grown up in weeds and grass, and on each board is the single word 'Rebel.'" Before long, 107 soldiers from North Carolina who had died in the capital during the war were on their way back to North Carolina. They were transported via steamer to Norfolk and then via train to Raleigh, where they lay in state in the capitol rotunda overnight. The next day, October 17, 1883, with much pomp and circumstance, the remains were taken to the Confederate section of Oakwood Cemetery and reinterred.

Work began anew on erecting monuments in 1883 when a statue of a soldier was dedicated in the Willow Dale Cemetery in Goldsboro. This was followed by monuments in the Cedar Grove Cemetery in New Bern in 1885; in Elmwood Cemetery in Charlotte and the Riverside Cemetery in Smithfield in 1887; and in Greensboro in the Green Hill Cemetery and in Washington at the Trinity Cemetery in 1888.

The 1880s also gave rise, on the Southern side, to the veterans' movement and, on the Northern side, to a renewal of already established veterans' groups. On the Northern side, the impetus to create a veterans' organization began even before the war ended. On April 14, 1865, Federal army officers serving under General William T. Sherman met while passing through Raleigh and

Members of the 35th United States Colored Troops gathered for a reunion in Plymouth, North Carolina, circa 1905. *Rhonda S. Gordon/North Carolina State Archives.*

created the Society of the Army of the Tennessee. Membership in the group was limited to officers who had served in the Army of the Tennessee, and the group continued to function through the 1910s. The largest organization of former Union soldiers, the Grand Army of the Republic, was created in Illinois in April 1866, founded upon the principles of "Fraternity, Charity and Loyalty." Each state comprised a department, and local organizations in towns and cities were known as posts. The North Carolina Department of the Grand Army of the Republic was organized on July 11, 1868, with eight posts, including ones in Wilmington and Raleigh. On December 2, 1872, the Department of North Carolina was disbanded due to lack of interest, and nationally, the Grand Army of the Potomac also ceased to exist. The 1880s brought new leadership, and the organization began to grow. The posts in North Carolina and Virginia were organized into one department. At its zenith in the 1890s, the Grand Army of the Republic had almost 500,000 members nationwide. There were a total of twenty-two Grand Army of the Republic posts in North Carolina, and in 1897, there were an estimated 400 members in the state. One of the most active and long-lasting posts was the Major General John F. Hartranft Post in Charlotte. Created in 1890, the Hartranft Post continued to exist through 1931. These Union veterans met annually with their Confederate counterparts to decorate the graves of Confederate soldiers in Charlotte on Confederate Memorial Day and then made their observances at the National Cemetery in Salisbury. Nationally, the Grand Army of the Republic held reunions each year, erected monuments, maintained homes for old soldiers, met frequently and, for a time in the late nineteenth century, was politically active. The Grand Army of the Republic ceased to exist in 1956 with the death of its last member.

Yet another annual act of commemoration was taking place in North Carolina. Beginning in 1865 in New Bern, African Americans began gathering on January 1 to celebrate and observe Emancipation Day. The special events included parades, speeches, the reading of Lincoln's proclamation and banquets. In many North Carolina communities with sizable African American populations, the celebrations continued for decades. Zebulon Baird Vance spoke in Raleigh on Emancipation Day in 1878, and the 1898 address, delivered by African American former congressman H.P. Cheatham, was attended by the governor, secretary of state and numerous other political leaders.

Former North Carolinians who served the Confederacy also created their own veterans' groups and commemorations. Just a few months after the war, officers of the 3rd North Carolina Troops met in Wilmington to reinter the remains of Lieutenant Colonel William Parsley, who was killed on April 6, 1865, during the Battle of Farmville, Virginia. While deciding the details of the reinterment, they chose to create the Third North Carolina Infantry Association. The association was originally only for officers, but after time, enlisted men were also admitted. The organization continued to exist through 1911.

A newspaper article in the *Raleigh News and Observer* in October 1881 invited Confederate veterans in attendance at the state fair to meet in a large hall for a two-hour reception. On the evening of October 12, "an informal meeting [was] held at the Yarborough House…by a number of ex-Confederates" who resolved to propose at the reunion the next day that a permanent Confederate veterans' organization be organized. The *News and Observer* reported on October 14 that the crowds numbered "some 500" participants at the scheduled 1:00 p.m. gathering. The meeting was called to order by former general William Cox, who called upon another former general, Thomas Clingman, as temporary chair. After some remarks, a call was made for a committee, which proposed the resolutions that had been adopted at the previous meeting at the Yarborough House. These resolutions called for the creation of the Society of Ex-Confederate Soldiers and Sailors of North Carolina, a suggestion that was met with agreement. Wharton Green, a former lieutenant colonel of the 2nd North Carolina Battalion, was elected president, and there was a vice-president for each of the eight districts, along with two members at large and a secretary. The society was called upon to meet at least once a year, usually coinciding with the state fair. Membership was open to anyone who produced "satisfactory evidence of honorable service in the Confederate army or navy." Many were called upon to make remarks, including Green, Captain Octavius Coke of the 32nd Virginia Infantry and General Cox. North Carolina governor Thomas Jarvis, himself a veteran of the 8th North Carolina State Troops, was soon spotted in the crowd and asked to make remarks. He spoke at considerable length, exhorting his fellow North Carolinians to "preserve a memorial of the part we played in the late war for futurity." By December 1881, the group had become known as the Confederate Survivors Association of North Carolina.

Confederate veterans gathered in 1911 at the home of Mrs. A.E. Woodbridge in Brevard. *Transylvania County Library Archives.*

Other veteran groups were soon springing up across the state to become involved in Memorial Day services, veteran activities and monument dedications. Former members of the Goldsboro Rifles marched in a Memorial Day parade in Goldsboro on May 10, 1882. A couple of weeks later, veterans from Company F, 24th North Carolina Troops, met in Smithfield and proposed a countywide reunion on July 21, 1882. More than five hundred veterans gathered in Wadesboro on July 22, 1882, to march in a parade and partake of a dinner on the grounds.

All across the South, former veterans were creating veteran organizations. In 1889, representatives from some of these groups met in Louisiana and formed the United Confederate Veterans. Former Confederate general John B. Gordon was named as the first commander in chief, the leader of the national organization. In March 1890, Gordon announced his staff, including several prominent North Carolinians: Robert F. Hoke was named inspector general, and among the aide-de-camps were Alfred Scales, Robert Vance and Robert Ransom. The "object and purpose of this organization will be strictly social, literary, historical and benevolent...to gather authentic data for an impartial history of the war...to preserve the relics or mementoes... [and] to care for the disabled and extend a hand to the needy." In 1892, North Carolina's Junius Daniels Camp in Raleigh met and voted to become

Cherokee Confederate soldiers, members of Thomas's Legion, attending a reunion in New Orleans in 1903. *North Carolina State Archives.*

part of the United Confederate Veterans. They also voted to send delegates to the national reunion being held in New Orleans in April. Slowly, the Confederate veteran organizations across the state began to join the United Confederate Veterans.

Each former Southern state constituted a division in the United Confederate Veterans, and local organizations were called camps. Often, camps were named after local Confederates, like the Nimrod Triplett Camp in Boone. Other camps, like the Major General William D. Pender Camp in Burnsville, chose the name of a beloved commander. Some chose geographical features, like the Camp Fear Camp in Wilmington. The North Carolina Division of the United Confederate Veterans was officially created in April 1892, and Edward Hall, former colonel of the 46th North Carolina Troops, was appointed the first commander.

Each camp normally held an annual reunion. Often these reunions were centered on May 10, the date adopted as Confederate Memorial or Decoration Day in North Carolina. Sometimes these reunions were local affairs, and at other times, whole regions of the state were invited. In August 1891, a reunion was held at the Blowing Rock Assembly Grounds on the Caldwell-Watauga County border. The event featured a band, several speakers and a parade of veterans. A massive outpouring of food from the citizens of the area kept many fed. An estimated 18,000 veterans, family members and community people attended this reunion. In 1892, the second statewide reunion was held in Wrightsville, near Wilmington. An estimated 1,500 veterans were expected to attend. It was not until 1895 that the Zebulon Baird Vance Camp in Asheville chose to join the national organization. By 1901, there were seventy United Confederate Veteran camps in North Carolina.

Other organizations sprang up alongside the United Confederate Veterans. In 1894, a group of ladies belonging to different memorial associations met in Nashville and formed the United Daughters of the Confederacy. Just a few months later, the widow of Lieutenant Colonel Parsley, around whom the first Confederate veterans' organization in North Carolina had been formed, organized the first United Daughters of the Confederacy chapter in North Carolina. The organization was known as the Cape Fear Chapter and was based in Wilmington. It was the third chapter organized in the United States. In April 1897, delegates from five different chapters in North Carolina met in Wilmington and created the North Carolina Division of the United Daughters of the Confederacy. Mrs. Parsley was elected the first president of the division. By 1901, there were thirty chapters in North Carolina, stretching from Wilmington to Asheville.

The funeral carriage of Jefferson Davis traveling through the streets of Raleigh. *North Carolina Museum of History.*

The real effort to honor or commemorate North Carolinians and the state's role really began in 1893 with a funeral. Former Confederate president Jefferson Davis had died in 1889 and was originally interred in New Orleans. After three years, the Davis family finally consented to allow his remains to be moved to Hollywood Cemetery in Richmond, Virginia. In late May 1893, the process began to transfer Davis's remains. Cities all along the route held their own funerals for the Confederate leader. There were six stops in North Carolina. In Greensboro, banks and stores were closed and flags flown at half-staff. Over five hundred schoolchildren dropped flowers on the coffin in Durham. Once the train reached Raleigh, a crowd of twenty thousand gathered to pay their respects as the funeral carriage passed through the streets. The coffin was placed in the state capitol, resting under the flag of the 5th North Carolina Troops. Thousands filed past, a considerable number considering the casket was only in the capitol rotunda for two hours. Davis's remains were soon back on the train, passing back through Durham and Greensboro before stopping for a short time in Reidsville, where a couple

Monuments in Raleigh. *Top, left to right*: Monument to Confederate soldiers and monument to Henry Wyatt, both on capitol grounds. *Bottom*: North Carolina Confederate Women's monument and unknown Tar Heel gravestone in Oakwood Cemetery. *Author's collection.*

of thousand men, women and children had gathered. After taking on water and fuel, the train continued on into Virginia.

May 1895 found another crowd lining the streets of Raleigh. An estimated thirty thousand gathered for the dedication of the monument on Union Square. Hundreds of veterans assembled, some marching under their faded banners. Different militia regiments were present, along with various other dignitaries. Widows of former generals, including Nancy Branch and Mary Ann Jackson, were on the platform. In due time, Julia Jackson Christian, the granddaughter of Stonewall Jackson, pulled the rope, and the covering on the monument slipped down to deafening cheers and the peal of bells.

With zeal, North Carolinians moved from erecting monuments honoring the dead to monuments that perpetuated the memory of the Confederacy. In most instances, the Daughters of the Confederacy took the lead in this effort at commemoration. In August 1902, a monument was dedicated in Columbia on the grounds of the courthouse in Tyrell County. Three years later, in 1905, the United Daughters of the Confederacy in Asheville unveiled three monuments on a single day, all on the courthouse grounds, a feat unrivaled to this day in the Tar Heel State. The primary monument was dedicated to the 60th North Carolina Troops, a regiment consisting almost

The monument to North Carolina soldiers at Gettysburg was dedicated in July 1929. *North Carolina Museum of History.*

entirely of Buncombe County men. The other two monuments, smaller in nature and erected by families, were to Thomas L. Clingman, former United States senator and Confederate brigadier general, and Colonel William B. Creasman, former commander of the 29th North Carolina Troops. In the 1910s and 1920s, monument dedication peaked, with over fifty monuments erected in North Carolina during those two decades. North Carolinians were also looking beyond their own borders. In 1905, monuments were dedicated to the North Carolina regiments that fought at Chickamauga. These were followed by Tar Heel monuments at Appomattox in 1905, Vicksburg in 1925 and Gettysburg in 1929.

In 1929, North Carolina hosted, for the only time, the national reunion of the United Confederate Veterans. About 3,500 veterans traveled from across the nation to attend the reunion. Concerts were presented, parades traveled through town and speeches and dances were given. One observer wrote, "Many [veterans who] seemed too feeble to walk any distance could shake a wicked foot when the music called for action." Two veterans, one from Texas and one from Missouri, passed away during the reunion. North Carolina governor O. Max Gardner spoke, among others. The reunion brought a total of 20,000 visitors to the Queen City, and before the veterans left, a plaque commemorating the event was dedicated at the auditorium that held the conventioneers.

The old veterans were quickly crossing over the river. North Carolina had done its best to care for its veterans since the end of the war. In 1867, the state, still impoverished by the war, began granting pensions to veterans who had lost a limb or were blind. This was followed by the pension act in 1885, which granted pensions to those who were disabled and indigent or who were destitute widows. There was a new pension act in 1901, opening the way for any Confederate veterans who could document their service, and their widows, to receive assistance from the state. The pensioners were divided up into four classes: the first-class members were totally disabled; second-class were those who had lost a leg above the knee or arm above the elbow; third-class were those who had lost a foot or leg below the knee or an arm below the elbow or had received a wound that made a limb useless; and fourth-class consisted of those who had lost an eye, were unfit for general labor or were widows. In 1901, first-class pensioners received seventy-two dollars per year, while fourth-class received thirty dollars. The 1901 Pension Act was modified several times, including once in 1927 when black men who had served in the Confederate army as cooks and wagoneers became eligible. All counties in North Carolina were required to have pensioner boards to help interview the applicants and facilitate the distribution of funds.

Many reunions featured drum and fife music. Here is the Lawrence O'Bryan Branch Drum and Fife Corps in 1909. *North Carolina Museum of History*.

In 1890, the state established a Soldiers Home in a rented house in Raleigh with five aged veterans. A year later, the home had almost doubled in size, to nine veterans, and had moved to Camp Russell, a former Spanish-American War training facility. The old Soldiers Home grew over time. New buildings and a hospital were added. There were 70 old soldiers at the home in 1901 and 209 in 1917. Each county was responsible for paying for the upkeep of veterans from that county. The facility closed in 1938, with 1,459 veterans passing through the doors. Likewise, there was a Confederate Women's Home established in 1913 in Fayetteville. The purpose of the home, according to the *North Carolina Manual*, "was to establish, maintain, and govern a home for deserving, needy and dependent wives and widows of North Carolina Confederate soldiers." In many instances, United Daughters of the Confederacy chapters adopted different rooms at the facility, which officially opened in November 1915. To live in the home, a woman had to be sixty-five years of age or older, impoverished and the wife, daughter or widow of a Confederate soldier. The home closed in 1981, even though there were still 7 occupants who had to be moved to other facilities.

North Carolina's last recognized Union veteran, Anderson Moore, briefly served in the 64th North Carolina Troops but later deserted and joined the 3rd

North Carolina Mounted (U.S.). He died in 1949 and is buried in Madison County. The state's last Confederate veteran, Sam Bennett, reportedly a member of the 58th North Carolina Troops, passed away on March 9, 1951, and is buried Mitchell County.

Even though all of North Carolina's soldiers are gone, along with their widows, the work of remembrance continues. The United Daughters of the Confederacy work on, their motto being "Lest it ever be forgotten." Other organizations have also been created, like the Sons of Confederate Veterans, formed in Richmond, Virginia, in 1896, and the Sons of Union Veterans of the Civil War, organized in 1881 by the Grand Army of the Republic. Both of these groups work to clean cemeteries, document the graves of soldiers, erect monuments and perpetuate the memory of North Carolina's Confederate and Union soldiers.

Chapter 9

Looking for the Civil War in North Carolina Today

One of the most interesting aspects of North Carolina and the Civil War is that it happened here. Large-scale battles were fought in the eastern third of the state, while numerous skirmishes and raids occurred in the mountains and the central portion of North Carolina served as a major supply source, along with a prison, for the Confederacy. Most local historical societies and museums have information and, at times, displays of artifacts dealing with the war, while many local libraries have resources on the events that took place within their specific area. However, there are a few places, both in North Carolina and in surrounding states, that hold special significance to those seeking to learn more.

Someone wanting to know more about the Civil War in North Carolina should naturally visit the state capitol in Raleigh. While the state legislators have moved into a nearby building, the governor still maintains an office in the old state capitol. The building was constructed in 1840 and survived the war. Today, the chambers of the House and Senate appear much as they did in the 1860s. On the grounds outside the capitol are numerous statues, like the ones honoring Henry Wyatt and the women of the Confederacy. The cannons flanking the large Confederate Monument were once at Fort Caswell. Across the street from the state capitol is the North Carolina Museum of History. This museum houses the largest collection of artifacts from the war, and various pieces of the collection are usually on display. A block away from the Museum of History is the North Carolina Department of Archives and History. Within its vaults are numerous records pertaining

Only the foundation and a few larger stones remain of the Fayetteville Arsenal today. It sits adjacent to the Museum of the Cape Fear in Fayetteville. *Author's collection.*

to the soldiers and civilians from North Carolina and their involvement during the Civil War. A few blocks away, on Oakwood Avenue, is the Historic Oakwood Cemetery. There are numerous war-related graves in Oakwood, including those of Brigadier General George B. Anderson; the boy colonel of the Confederacy, Henry Kidd Burgwyn; Major General Robert F. Hoke; Governor William W. Holden; and his nemesis, Governor Jonathan Worth. Along with these is a large Confederate section containing the dead from the Pettigrew Hospital, moved right after the war, the Gettysburg dead and Tar Heel dead from Arlington National Cemetery. Also worth a visit is the Raleigh National Cemetery, on Rock Quarry Road, the former site of the Confederate Hospital and Cemetery.

On the coast, Wilmington has much to offer the visitor. Much of wartime Wilmington survives. Blockade runners tied up along the waterfront to unload their cargoes or to take on North Carolina cotton for export. On the steps of the 1858 city hall—now the Thalian Hall, a playhouse—Mayor John Dawson surrendered to Major General Alfred H. Terry on February 22, 1865. St. James Episcopal Church on Market Street was used as a Federal hospital. A visit to the Cape Fear Museum is also a great way to learn more about Wilmington's wartime past. Oakdale Cemetery on Fifteenth Street contains the graves of Confederates killed during the battles for Fort Fisher. There is a large open plot where those who died during the 1862 yellow fever epidemic are interred, along with the graves of Confederate naval officer John Maffitt and famed spy Rose O'Neal Greenhow. To the south of Wilmington, between the Cape Fear River and the Atlantic Ocean, is Fort Fisher, a major earthwork fortification that was the last major stronghold of the Confederacy. On the west side of the Cape Fear River is Fort Anderson, another impressive earthen fortification, located at Old Brunswick Town. On Oak Island, across from Southport, are the remnants of Fort Caswell, a masonry fort constructed prior to the war. It is currently owned by the North Carolina Baptist Assembly.

North Carolina's other masonry fortification, Fort Macon, is located to the north, near Morehead City. Fort Macon was repaired after the war and was the second piece of property acquired by North Carolina to be used as a state park. Near Morehead City is the grave of Emeline Pigott, and in Beaufort, visitors should visit the North Carolina Maritime Museum.

Much of Roanoke Island, in Roanoke Sound, hosted positions for Confederate and Union troops in 1862. There are numerous historical markers and trail signs across the island. The Federals captured the old coastal town of New Bern after taking Roanoke Island. Part of the battlefield,

Sherman and Johnston met at the Bennett Place in April 1865. *Author's collection.*

about five miles below the town, has been preserved. In the town, a visitor can find numerous wartime-related sites, including the New Bern Civil War Museum on Pollock Street, the New Bern Academy on Hancock Street, the Attmore-Oliver House on Broad Street and First Presbyterian Church on New Street, which was used as a hospital and lookout during the war. Cedar Grove Cemetery has graves of Confederates who died during the Battle of New Bern, while the New Bern National Cemetery has the graves of Federal soldiers from the battle. The Fireman's Museum on Hancock Street also has wartime artifacts.

Kinston is a great place to visit when looking for information about North Carolina and the war. The area witnessed several wartime battles, along with the hanging of Union prisoners by General George Pickett in 1864. In Kinston, visitors must see the recovered hull and artifacts from the CSS *Neuse* before heading over a few blocks to visit the CSS *Neuse II*, a full-size re-creation of the famed ironclad.

On March 15, 1865, Federal and Confederate forces clashed just below Fayetteville, at Averasboro. Part of the battlefield has been preserved, and there is a museum. In Fayetteville, one can visit the Cross Creek Cemetery, where there are numerous Confederate graves, along with the first Confederate monument erected in North Carolina after the war. Also very worthy of a visit is the Museum of the Cape Fear, where a visitor will find not only artifacts from the Civil War, but also on the grounds are the remains of the United State Arsenal, used by Confederates to manufacture rifles before being torched by Sherman's men.

If travelers follow the path of Sherman, after stops at Averasboro and Fayetteville, they should visit the Bentonville Battle State Historic Site, the premier Civil War site in North Carolina. The Confederates tried to stop Sherman's army here in March 1865, but overwhelming Federal numbers kept the Confederates from following up their initial successes. Preservation at Bentonville began in the 1960s, with the acquisition of 51 acres and the Harper House, which had served as a field hospital. Thanks to the work of various preservation groups, like the Civil War Trust and the Bentonville Battlefield Historical Association, over 1,300 acres of the battlefield are currently protected from development.

One other great site in the eastern part of North Carolina is located near Hamilton, on the Roanoke River: Fort Branch. Construction began on the earthen fort in February 1862, and it was later expanded into works that contained eleven guns with obstructions, including torpedoes in the river. The fort was abandoned in February 1865. The site is privately owned,

Located on the Bentonville Battlefield, the Harper House was used as a hospital during the battle. *Author's collection.*

but numerous living history programs, and an annual reenactment every November, allow people to access the restored site.

Traveling west out of Raleigh will take one past the Bennett Place in Durham. The reconstructed farmhouse sits on the site of the meeting between Generals Joseph E. Johnston (CS) and William T. Sherman (U.S.). In April 1865, Johnston surrendered all of his forces to Sherman, and the official war in North Carolina came to a close. The site has a great museum, and frequent living histories are conducted throughout the year. Just south of Durham is Chapel Hill, the site of the first public university in North Carolina. Various high-ranking Confederates were educated at the university, including Zebulon Baird Vance, state senator William W. Avery, U.S. senator Thomas L. Clingman and Major General Bryan Grimes. Those doing research often visit the Southern Historical Collection on campus, which contains numerous collections of letters from prominent Confederate and Union soldiers and politicians. Also on campus is a Confederate monument, named Silent Sam, dedicated to university graduates who served in the war. An essential stop for the researcher is the Perkins Library on Duke University's campus in Durham.

The Hall of Memory is located in the Oakwood Cemetery in Raleigh. *Author's collection.*

A visit to the Greensboro Historical Museum in Greensboro is the highlight of any trip. The museum, housed on the site of a Presbyterian church used as a hospital after the Battle of Bentonville, also houses the Murphy Confederate Weapons Collection, one of the best private Confederate firearms collections in the world. While in Greensboro, one can stop by the Green Hill Cemetery and its Confederate monument, dedicated in 1888. Interred at Green Hill is Confederate general Alfred Moore Scales, later a governor of North Carolina.

Just a little farther west is Winston-Salem, which was two separate communities in the 1860s. Members of the celebrated band of the 26th North Carolina Troops came from Salem, and some are buried in the Salem Cemetery, along with Brigadier General William R. Boggs. Also in Salem, at the intersection of Main Street and Brookstown Avenue, is a large coffeepot where it is rumored that Confederates hid when Union forces under General Stoneman arrived in April 1865.

Stoneman visited numerous towns and communities on his raid in March and April 1865, including Boone, Wilkesboro, Mount Airy, High Point, Lexington and Salisbury. Near the latter, he was turned back by local forces at Fort York on Deep River. Stoneman's mounted soldiers then turned west, moving through Statesville, Taylorsville, Lenoir, Morganton, Lincolnton, Hendersonville and finally Asheville.

At Salisbury, Stoneman hoped to release the Federal prisoners quartered there, but he found them gone. Nothing today remains of the prison, but one can visit the Salisbury National Cemetery, with its monuments to Pennsylvania and Maine soldiers. Among the thousands interred at Salisbury is Lorenzo Denning, captured after the attack on the *Albemarle*. He probably never knew he had been awarded the Medal of Honor. Also in Salisbury is one of the most beautiful Confederate monuments in the state. Located on Church and Innes Streets, the monument was dedicated in 1909, with Mrs. Stonewall Jackson as one of the special guests. Also in the town is the Old English Cemetery, which holds the remains of Governor John W. Ellis and Colonel Charles Fisher. Fisher was killed at the Battle of First Manassas, and Ellis died while in office in 1861.

Charlotte is seldom mentioned in most Civil War histories, but it has a rich past. It was the site of a military hospital and, for a short time toward

Dedicated on June 10, 1909, the Confederate monument in Salisbury depicts a dying Confederate soldier being supported and crowned by Fame. *North Carolina Museum of History.*

Salisbury National Cemetery contains the graves of thousands of Union soldiers and sympathizers. *Author's collection.*

the end of the war, a prison. The Confederate Naval Yard was established on East Trade Street after the fall of Norfolk, Virginia, and there is a state historic marker denoting the fact. There was also a North Carolina Powder Manufacturing facility on Tuckaseegee Ford Road, the Confederate States Acid Works and a facility to manufacture military clothing. Jefferson Davis spent time in Charlotte while fleeing from Federal forces at the close of the war, holding his last full cabinet meeting on South Tryon Street. Much of the surviving Confederate archives from Richmond were captured in Charlotte. Elmwood Cemetery in Charlotte contains a Confederate monument, around which are the graves of men who died in Charlotte during the war. Mrs. Stonewall Jackson lived off South Graham Street after the war, and to the north of town, Confederate lieutenant general Daniel H. Hill is buried in the Davidson College Cemetery.

Much interesting Civil War history can be found along the I-26 corridor in the western part of North Carolina. Just below Hendersonville is the Carl Sandburg Home National Historic Site. But there is more to the place than just the home of a Pulitzer Prize–winning biographer of Abraham Lincoln. Sandburg's home, Connemara, was also the home of Christopher Memminger, Confederate secretary of the treasury from 1861 to 1864.

Memminger is buried not far away, along with other Confederates, at the St. John in the Wilderness Episcopal Church. To the north is Asheville, once considered for the Confederate capital because of its remote location. The 1840 Smith-McDowell House, on Victoria Road, is a great place to start a tour of local sites. On the campus of the University of North Carolina at Asheville are the remains of Confederate breastworks that once held off portions of Stoneman's command. Riverside Cemetery, off Pearson Drive, is the final resting place of Governor Zebulon Baird Vance, his brother Brigadier General Robert B. Vance and Brigadier General Thomas L. Clingman, along with other notable Confederates. Brigadier General Andrew J. McGonnigle (U.S.), a staff officer serving General Philip Sheridan who was wounded during the Battle of Cedar Creek, Virginia, in October 1864 and a winner of the Medal of Honor, is also buried at Riverside. Just a little farther north of Asheville, but still in Buncombe County, is the Zebulon Baird Vance Birthplace State Historic Site. While the cabins themselves are not original, they were reconstructed around the original chimneys. There is a museum on site that contains artifacts from Vance's life.

A little farther west, on the border of the Great Smoky Mountains National Park, is the town of Cherokee and the Museum of the Cherokee Indians. The museum has an exhibit on Thomas's Legion of Cherokee Indians and Highlanders, a rather unique organization in Confederate service.

For a visitor traveling outside the Tar Heel State, there is much to see. While some of the land where North Carolina regiments fought has been lost to development, like the Chantilly battlefield near Washington, D.C., and some of it is not preserved, like Hanover Court House in Virginia, one can travel to the National Battlefield Parks like Manassas, Fredericksburg, Chancellorsville, Gettysburg, the Wilderness, Spotsylvania, Reams Station, the Petersburg trenches and Appomattox and, with the help of guides or map books, walk the grounds where Tar Heel soldiers trod and fought. Monuments erected in honor of North Carolina can be found at Gettysburg, Vicksburg and South Mountain, while individual soldiers are honored at Antietam and Cedar Mountain. A few regiments, like the 26th North Carolina at Gettysburg and the 58th North Carolina at Chickamauga, have their own monuments.

We can learn much about the most tumultuous period of North Carolina's history by visiting the sites associated with the time period, studying the artifacts at museums that they left behind and reading the letters they sent back home.

Selected Bibliography

Anderson, Lucy. *North Carolina Women of the Confederacy.* N.p.: North Carolina Division, United Daughters of the Confederacy, 1926.

Angley, Wilson. *A History of Fort Johnson on the Lower Cape Fear River.* Wilmington, NC: Broadfoot Publishing Company, 1996.

Auman, William T. "Neighbor against Neighbor: The Inner Civil War in the Central Counties of Confederate North Carolina." PhD dissertation. University of North Carolina, 1988.

Barrett, John G. *The Civil War in North Carolina.* Chapel Hill: University of North Carolina Press, 1963.

———. *North Carolina as a Civil War Battleground.* Raleigh: North Carolina Department of Cultural Resources, 1991.

Bisher, Catherine W. "'A Strong Force of Ladies': Women, Politics, and Confederate Memorial Associations in Nineteenth-Century Raleigh." *North Carolina Historical Review* 77, no. 4 (October 2000): 455–91.

Blair, Jayne E. *Tragedy at Montpelier: The Untold Story of Ten Confederate Deserters from North Carolina.* Westminster, MD: Heritage Books, 2003.

Bradley, Mark L. *The Battle of Bentonville: Last Stand in the Carolinas.* Campbell, CA: Savas Publishing Company, 1996.

———. *Bluecoats and Tarheels: Soldiers and Civilians in Reconstruction North Carolina.* Lexington: University Press of Kentucky, 2009.

———. *This Astounding Close: The Road to Bennett Place.* Chapel Hill: University of North Carolina Press, 2000.

Branch, Paul. *Fort Macon: A History.* Charleston, SC: The Nautical & Aviation Publishing Company of America, 1999.

Brown, Louis A. *The Salisbury Prison.* Wilmington, NC: Broadfoot, 1992.

Brown, Norman D. *Edward Stanly: Whiggery's Tar Heel "Conqueror."* Tuscaloosa: University of Alabama Press, 1974.

Burton, Jesse. *Statesman of the Lost Cause: Jefferson Davis and His Cabinet.* New York: Literary Guild of America, 1939.

Clark, Walter, ed. *Histories of the Several Regiments and Battalions from North Carolina in the Great War 1861–1865.* Goldsboro, NC: Nash Brothers Book and Job Printers, 1901.

Cole, J. Timothy, and Bradley R. Foley. *Collett Leventhorpe: The English Confederate.* Jefferson, NC: McFarland and Company, 2007.

Collins, Donald E. *The Death and Resurrection of Jefferson Davis.* New York: Bowman and Littlefield Publishers, Inc., 2005.

Conner, R.D.W. *North Carolina Manual.* Raleigh, NC: Edwards & Broughton Printing Company, 1921.

Crabtree, Beth G., and James W. Patton, eds. *"Journal of a Secesh Lady": The Diary of Catherine Ann Devereux Edmondston, 1860–1866.* Raleigh: Division of Archives and History, North Carolina Department of Cultural Resources, 1979.

Crow, Vernon H. *Storm in the Mountains: Thomas' Confederate Legion of Cherokee Indians and Mountaineers.* Cherokee, NC: Press of the Museum of the Cherokee Indians, 1982.

Dedmond, Francis B. "Harvey Davis's Unpublished Civil War Diary and the Story of Company D of the First North Carolina Cavalry." *Appalachian Journal* (Summer 1986): 368–407.

Dedmondt, Glenn. *The Flags of Civil War North Carolina.* Gretna, LA: Pelican Publishing Co., 2003.

Dowd, Clement. *The Life of Zebulon B. Vance.* Charlotte, NC: Observer Printing and Publishing, 1897.

Durrill, Wayne K. *War of Another Kind: A Southern Community in the Great Rebellion.* Oxford, UK: Oxford University Press, 1990.

Escott, Raul D. *Many Excellent People: Power and Privilege in North Carolina, 1850–1900.* Chapel Hill: University of North Carolina Press, 1985.

Five Points in the Record of North Carolina in the Great War of 1861–5. Goldsboro, NC: Nash Brothers, 1904.

Foner, Eric. *A Short History of Reconstruction.* New York: Harper and Row, 1990.

Fonvielle, Chris E., Jr. *The Wilmington Campaign: Last Rays of Departing Hope.* Mechanicsburg, PA: Stackpole Books, 2001.

Gragg, Rod. *Confederate Goliath: The Battle of Fort Fisher.* Baton Rouge: Louisiana State University Press, 1991.

Greenwood, Janette T. *On the Home Front: Charlotte During the Civil War.* Charlotte, NC: Mint Museum, 1982.

Griffin, Clarence W. *History of the Old Tryon and Rutherford Counties.* Asheville, NC: Miller Printing Company, 1937.

Hardy, Michael C. *The Fifty-eighth North Carolina Troops: Tar Heels in the Army of Tennessee.* Jefferson, NC: McFarland and Company, 2010.

————. *Remembering North Carolina's Confederates.* Charleston, SC: Arcadia Publishing, 2008.

————. *A Short History of Old Watauga County.* Boone, NC: Parkway Publishing, 2005.

————. *The Thirty-seventh North Carolina Troops: Tar Heels in the Army of Northern Virginia.* Jefferson, NC: McFarland and Company, 2003.

Harris, William C. *William Woods Holden: Firebrand of North Carolina Politics.* Baton Rouge: Louisiana State University Press, 1987.

Hartley, Chris J. *Stoneman's Raid, 1865.* Winston-Salem, NC: John F. Blair, 2010.

Hilderman, Walter C., III *They Went into the Fight Cheering: Confederate Conscription in North Carolina.* Boone, NC: Parkway Publishers, 2005.

Hill, D.H., Jr. *Confederate Military History: North Carolina.* Atlanta, 1899.

Hinds, John W. *The Hunt for the Albemarle: Anatomy of a Gunboat War.* Shippensburg, PA: Burd Street Press, 2001.

Inscoe, John C., and Gordon McKinney. *The Heart of Confederate Appalachia: Western North Carolina in the Civil War.* Chapel Hill: University of North Carolina Press, 2000.

Jeffrey, Thomas E. *Thomas Lanier Clingman: Fire Eater from the Carolina Mountains.* Athens: University of Georgia Press, 1998.

Jewell, M., and Mary Green Matthews Sink. *Pathfinders Past and Present: A History of Davidson County, North Carolina.* N.p.: Hall Printing Co., 1972.

Johnson, Clint. *Touring the Carolina's Civil War Sites.* Winston-Salem, NC: John F. Blair, 1996.

Johnston, Frontis W., ed. *The Papers of Zebulon Baird Vance, 1843–1862.* Raleigh, NC: State Department of Archives and History, 1963.

Jordan, Weymoth T., Jr., Louis H. Manarin, et. al., eds. *North Carolina Troops, 1861–1865.* 17 vols. Raleigh: North Carolina Department of Archives and History, 1961 to present.

Joslyn, Mauriel Phillips. *Captives Immortal.* Shippensburg, PA: White Mane Publishing, 1996.

Kruman, Marc W. *Parties and Politics in North Carolina, 1836–1865*. Baton Rouge: Louisiana State University Press, 1983.

Long, E.B. *The Civil War Day by Day, An Almanac 1861–1865*. New York: Doubleday & Company, 1971.

MacKethan, Mrs. Edwin R. *Chapter Histories, North Carolina Division, United Daughters of the Confederacy, 1897–1947*. N.p.: North Carolina Division, United Daughters of the Confederacy, 1947.

Mallison, Fred M. *The Civil War on the Outer Banks*. Jefferson, NC: McFarland and Company, 1998.

Manarin, Louis H. *Onslow County During the Civil War*. N.p., 1982.

Mast, Greg. *State Troops and Volunteers*. Raleigh: North Carolina Department of Cultural Resources, Division of Archives and History, 1995.

McCrary, Mary Jane. *Transylvania Beginnings: A History*. Easley, SC: Southern Historical Press, 1984.

McGee, David H. "'Hone and Friends': Kinship, Community, and Elite Women in Caldwell County, North Carolina, during the Civil War." *North Carolina Historical Review* 74, no. 4 (October 1997): 363–88.

————. "'On the Edge of the Crater': The Transformation of Raleigh, North Carolina During the Civil War." PhD dissertation. University of Georgia, 1999.

McKinney, Gordon B. *Zeb Vance: North Carolina's Civil War Governor and Gilded Age Political Leader*. Chapel Hill: University of North Carolina Press, 2004.

Meekins, Alex Christopher. *Elizabeth City, North Carolina and the Civil War*. Charleston, SC: The History Press, 2007.

Official Records of the Union and Confederate Navies in the War of the Rebellion. 30 vols. Washington, D.C.: U.S. Government Printing Office, 1894–1922.

Paludan, Phillip Shaw. *Victims: A True Story of the Civil War*. Knoxville: University of Tennessee Press, 1981.

Poteat, R. Matthew. *Henry Toole Clark: Civil War Governor of North Carolina*. Jefferson, NC: McFarland and Company, 2009.

Powell, William S. *North Carolina Through Four Centuries*. Chapel Hill: University of North Carolina Press, 1989.

Reid, Richard M. *Freedom for Themselves: North Carolina's Black Soldiers in the Civil War Era*. Chapel Hill: University of North Carolina Press, 2008.

Robinson, Blackwell, and Alexander R. Stoesen. *The History of Guilford County, North Carolina, to 1980*. N.p.: Guilford County Bicentennial Commission, 1980.

Sitterson, Joseph C. *The Secession Movement in North Carolina*. Chapel Hill: University of North Carolina Press, 1939.

Smith, S.L. *North Carolina's Confederate Monuments and Memorials.* Raleigh: NC Division, United Daughters of the Confederacy, 1941.

Sprunt, James. *Chronicles of the Cape Fear River: 1660–1916.* Raleigh, NC: Edwards and Broughton Printing Co., 1916.

Trotter, William R. *Bushwhackers! The Mountains.* Winston-Salem, NC: John F. Blair, 1989.

———. *Ironclads and Columbiads.* Winston-Salem, NC: John F. Blair, 1989.

———. *Silk Flags and Cold Steel.* Winston-Salem, NC: John F. Blair, 1989.

Tucker, Glenn. *Zeb Vance: Champion of Personal Freedom.* New York: Bobbs-Merrill Company, 1965.

U.S. Congress. "Testimony Taken by the Joint Committee to Inquire into the Condition of Affairs in the Late Insurrectionary States: North Carolina." *Senate Report No. 41, Part 2.* 42nd Congress, 2nd Session.

Van Noppen, Ina W., and John J. van Noppen. *Western North Carolina Since the Civil War.* Boone, NC: Appalachian Consortium Press, 1973.

Vincent, Tom. "'Evidence of Woman's Loyalty, Perseverance, and Fidelity': Confederate Soldiers' Monuments in North Carolina, 1865–1914." *North Carolina Historical Review* 73, no. 1 (January 2006): 61–90.

Weathers, Henry L. *Our Heritage: A History of Cleveland County.* Shelby, NC: Shelby's Daily Star, 1976.

Weaver, Jeffrey. *The 5th and 7th Battalions North Carolina Cavalry and the 6th North Carolina Cavalry.* Lynchburg, VA: H.E. Howard, 1995.

Wise, Stephen R. *Lifeline of the Confederacy: Blockade Running During the Civil War.* Columbia: University of South Carolina Press, 1991.

Wood, Richard E. "Port Town at War: Wilmington, North Carolina, 1860–1865." PhD dissertation. Florida State University, 1976.

Zuber, Richard L. *Jonathan Worth: A Biography of a Southern Unionist.* Chapel Hill: University of North Carolina Press, 1965.

———. *North Carolina During Reconstruction.* Raleigh, NC: State Department of Archives and History, 1969.

About the Author

Award-winning author and historian Michael C. Hardy has penned numerous books, articles and blog posts on North Carolina and the Civil War. In 2010, he was honored as the Historian of the Year by the North Carolina Society of Historians. He lives with his family in western North Carolina, near the famous Grandfather Mountain.

Visit us at
www.historypress.net